THE ORIENTAL INSTITUTE OF THE UNIVERSITY OF CHICAGO

STUDIES IN ANCIENT ORIENTAL CIVILIZATION · NO. 32

"Learn hence for ancient rules a just esteem. . . ."

Alexander Pope, *Essay on Criticism* i 139

PATTERNS
IN THE EARLY POETRY
OF ISRAEL

BY STANLEY GEVIRTZ

THE ORIENTAL INSTITUTE OF THE UNIVERSITY OF CHICAGO

STUDIES IN ANCIENT ORIENTAL CIVILIZATION · NO. 32

THE UNIVERSITY OF CHICAGO PRESS · CHICAGO · ILLINOIS

International Standard Book Number: 0-226-62405-6
Library of Congress Catalog Card Number: 73-80091

THE UNIVERSITY OF CHICAGO PRESS, CHICAGO 60637
THE UNIVERSITY OF CHICAGO PRESS, LTD., LONDON

TO MY PARENTS
MORRIS AND FANNIE GEVIRTZ

זכרונם לברכה

TABLE OF CONTENTS

LIST OF ABBREVIATIONS

AOF	Archiv für Orientforschung (Berlin, 1923——).
AJSL	The American journal of Semitic languages and literatures (Chicago etc., 1884–1941)
ANET	PRITCHARD, J. B. (ed.) Ancient Near Eastern texts relating to the Old Testament (2d ed.; Princeton, 1955).
ARM	Archives royales de Mari (Musée du Louvre. Département des antiquités orientales. Textes cunéiformes XXII——) (Paris, 1941——).
BASOR	American Schools of Oriental Research. Bulletin (South Hadley, Mass., 1919——).
BDB	BROWN, F., DRIVER, S. R., and BRIGGS, C. (eds.) A Hebrew and English lexicon of the Old Testament (Oxford, 1907).
BH	KITTEL, RUDOLF. (ed.) Biblia Hebraica (7th ed.; Stuttgart, 1951).
BMS	KING, L. W. Babylonian magic and sorcery (London, 1896).
CAD	Chicago. University. Oriental Institute. The Assyrian Dictionary (Chicago, 1956——).
CBQ	Catholic biblical quarterly (Washington, D.C., 1939——).
GKC	Gesenius' Hebrew grammar, as edited and enlarged by the late E. KAUTZSCH . . . 2d English ed. rev. in accordance with the 28th German ed. (1909) by A. E. COWLEY (Oxford, 1910).
HSCP	Harvard studies in classical philology (Cambridge, Mass., 1890——).
JAOS	American Oriental Society. Journal (Boston etc., 1849——).
Jastrow, Dictionary	JASTROW, MARCUS. A dictionary of the Targumim, the Talmud Babli and Yerushalmi, and the Midrashic literature (2 vols.; New York, 1950).
JBL	Journal of biblical literature (Philadelphia etc., 1881——).
JJS	Journal of Jewish studies (Cambridge, 1948——).
JNES	Journal of Near Eastern studies (Chicago, 1942——).
MAD	Chicago. University. Oriental Institute. Materials for the Assyrian Dictionary (3 vols.; Chicago, 1952–61).
Mél. Dussaud	Mélanges syriens offerts à Monsieur René Dussaud (Bibliothèque archéologique et historique XXX [2 vols.; Paris, 1939]).
PRU· II	Le palais royal d'Ugarit. II. Textes en cunéiformes alphabétiques des archives est, ouest, et centrales, par CHARLES VIROLLEAUD (Mission de Ras Shamra VII [Paris, 1957]).
RA	Revue d'assyriologie et d'archéologie orientale (Paris, 1884——).
Symb. Kosch.	Symbolae ad iura Orientis antiqui pertinentes Paulo Koschaker dedicatae . . . (Studia et documenta ad iura Orientis antiqui pertinentia II [Leiden, 1939]).

PROLOGUE

THIS monograph consists of a series of fresh studies of several biblical Hebrew poems that are related by virtue of the antiquity generally accorded them. These studies find their unity, also, in a method of investigation which aims at the elucidation of the individual texts through an examination of a particular stylistic device found to have been employed in them. No claim is made for this "approach" as being the sole legitimate procedure allowable in reading these or any other biblical Hebrew poems. It is strongly suggested, however, that a greater appreciation of the Hebrew poet's craft may thereby be had and that the reader may thus find himself afforded an opportunity for acquiring a clearer recognition of the individual poem's form and content.

In so far as the discussion of these several poetic works proceeds from an examination and a demonstration of the poets' use of a very specific literary convention to the more fundamental questions of meaning, rather than the reverse, the charge may well be leveled that there is here a rather serious breach of literary-critical technique. But the poetry of any given language—and, perhaps, every given poem—imposes upon the student its own emphases and its own logic, which may be discovered, I am convinced, only by close attention to minute details of style. These alone will not explain the "poetry" of the literary work; they cannot. Language, however poetically significant, however conventional, however restricted to poetic use, is but the medium through which the poet composes his poem; it is but an element of the poetic form, not the form itself.[1] Yet, in any consideration of a poetic tradition whose basic forms are still so energetically debated—and therefore, by implication, so ill-defined—as those of biblical Hebrew poetry, the isolation of any demonstrably traditional apparatus employed by the poets must find its place.

This little book, then, is about a tradition in Hebrew poetic composition and the patterns woven of this tradition by the biblical poets. It restricts itself to these, in large measure, because such patterns can, with reasonable precision, be traced and because the study of these patterns can increase one's understanding of the poems. It fails to take into account, for example, those patterns that are based on metrical considerations, and questions of meter find

[1] Cf. Elder Olson, "William Empson, Contemporary Criticism and Poetic Diction," *Critics and Criticism* (ed. R. S. Crane; Chicago, 1952) pp. 55 f., 68 f.

1

no place in the ensuing discussions of the individual poetic texts.[2] I feel that, while the existence of meter in biblical Hebrew poetry is highly probable and certainly cannot as yet be categorically denied, it has yet to be convincingly demonstrated. Metrical analysis, still dubious in the extreme, can add little to our understanding of a poem's content.

The history of the study of Hebrew poetry has been marked by two major discoveries. In his lectures published in 1753 under the title *De Sacra Poesi Hebraeorum Praelectiones Academicae*,[3] (Bishop) Robert Lowth described the principal means by which the biblical Hebrew poems appeared to have been fashioned and termed it *parallelismus membrorum*.[4] From that time, parallelism as the dominant stylistic feature of biblical Hebrew poetry has never seriously been questioned. With but minor variations, additions, and corrections to Lowth's initial observations concerning three varieties of parallelism, however, scholars apparently considered the matter of parallelistic structure essentially closed and busied themselves chiefly with questions of prosody.[5]

Then, in the early 1930's, with the decipherment of a substantial body of poetic texts recovered from the ruins of ancient Ugarit, a new impetus was given to the study of Old Testament and related literature. The poetic texts, in their extant form dating to the fourteenth century B.C.E., were found to have been composed in a language closely related—from a lexical point of view at least—to biblical Hebrew, though preserving several archaic elements not present in the latter as well as several divergent morphological features.[6] More importantly in the present context, it was found that the parallelistic structures evident in the Ugaritic poems were in all significant respects virtually identical with those known from Old Testament poetry. Still more central to

[2] A brief statement concerning the difficulties and possibilities of metrical analysis, as I view them, may be found on pp. 12–14.

[3] Chaps. iii and xix. The edition available to me is the translation by G. Gregory, *Lectures on the Sacred Poetry of the Hebrews* (with notes of Professor Michaelis *et al.*; London, 1847); also, and in greater detail, R. Lowth, *Isaiah: A New Translation with a Preliminary Dissertation*. The edition in my possession is the tenth and is dated 1833.

[4] For the recognition of this feature in periods prior to Lowth, on the part of Ibn Ezra and David Qimḥi, see the convenient summary of George Buchanan Gray, *The Forms of Hebrew Poetry* (London, 1915) particularly pp. 17 f.

[5] For a review of the more significant studies of Hebrew poetry since the appearance of Lowth's work, see the recent survey presented by T. H. Robinson, "Hebrew Poetic Form: The English Tradition," *Congress Volume, Copenhagen, 1953* (*VT* "Supplement" I [Leiden, 1953]) pp. 128–49.

[6] It would serve little purpose here to enter the debate on whether Ugaritic is or is not to be included among the Canaanite dialects. For arguments pro and con see particularly H. L. Ginsberg, *Orientalia* V (1936) 176–80; W. F. Albright, *CBQ* VII (1945) 14–18; A. Goetze, *Language* XVII (1941) 127–38; J. Cantineau, *Syria* XIII (1932) 164–69; *idem*, *Syria* XXI (1940) 38–61; *idem*, *Semitica* III (1950) 21–34; J. Friedrich, *Scientia* LXXXIV (1949) 220–23; N. H. Tur-Sinai, *Tarbiz* XXIII (1952) 143–45; E. Ullendorff, *Tarbiz* XXIV (1954–55) 121–25; I. J. Gelb, *Journal of Cuneiform Studies* XV (1961) 42.

the concerns of the present work was the recognition of a poetic diction common to the two literatures. Specific "pairs" of words in fixed parallel relationship were found to occur in both Ugaritic and Hebrew literature with such frequency and regularity as to preclude the possibility of coincidence, while the differences in age and locale excluded the possibility of direct borrowing.

It is to Professor H. L. Ginsberg that we owe this second major discovery, namely that the poets of ancient Syria and Palestine had at their command a body of conventionally fixed pairs of words upon which they might freely draw in the construction of their literary compositions. Ginsberg, in his characteristically concise phraseology, dubbed this phenomenon "the regular stock-in-trade of Canaanite poets."[7]

This observation and the comparative technique were exploited most fully by the late Professor Umberto [Moshe David] Cassuto in a series of studies culminating in his book *The Goddess Anath*[8] and continued by his (one-time) student, now Professor Moshe Held.[9] By isolating the pairs of fixed parallel words in the Ugaritic texts and locating these same pairs in biblical Hebrew poems they marshaled a significantly large array of irrefutable evidence in support of the theory that the two literatures, despite the difference in their age, locale, and stage of linguistic development, were in reality not two distinct literatures but merely represented two branches of a common, Syro-Palestinian, literary tradition. To this was added evidence culled from certain of the ᶜAmarnah letters[10]—letters written in learned Akkadian to the Egyptian court by Canaanite scribes of the fourteenth century B.C.E.—as well as from the few extant Canaanite royal inscriptions.[11]

In view of the impressive and ever-increasing body of evidence, the existence and continuity of a poetic tradition in Syria and Palestine of the second and first millenniums B.C.E., whatever may prove to be the *linguistic position* of

---

[7] See *Orientalia* V 171–72.

[8] הָאֵלָה עֲנָת (Jerusalem, 1953). For his earlier studies see *Tarbiz* XIII (1942) 197–212 and XIV (1942) 1–10 and *Leshonenu* XV (1947) 97–102.

[9] *Leshonenu* XVIII (1953) 144–60.

[10] Cassuto, *Tarbiz* XIV (1942) 9, has pointed to the parallelism of the phrases "to rejoice the heart" // "to brighten the eyes" occurring in Ps. 19:9 and in the ᶜAmarnah letters 142:7–10 and 144:14–18. [See now, S. Gevirtz, in *JNES* 32 (1973) pp. 99–104; *idem*, in *Orientalia* n.s. 43/1–2 (1973).]

[11] E.g. the parallelism "break/strip away the scepter of judicial authority" // "overturn the throne of dominion" is known from the Aḥiram inscription (*Syria* V [1924] 137) and from Ugaritic (*UM* 49 VI 28–29); the parallelism נשא // עָמַס, "carry away" // "bear away," is found in Isa. 46:3 and appears as well in the Eshmunᶜazar inscription (*Corpus Inscriptionum Semiticarum* I [1881] No. 3, line 7, Pl. II); and the parallelism רזן // מֶלֶךְ, "king" // "ruler," known to occur six times in biblical Hebrew verse (Judg. 5:3; Hab. 1:10; Ps. 2:2; Prov. 8:15, 14:28, 31:4) has appeared in the Azitawada inscription (col. iii 12). [See now, J. C. Greenfield, in *Near Eastern Studies in Honor of William Foxwell Albright*, ed. by H. Goedicke (Baltimore and London, 1971) pp. 253–68.]

Ugaritic, can no longer be open to doubt. But the use of this finding has, until now, been virtually restricted to such comparative studies as have been noted above; and no attempt, as far as I am aware, has been made to apply this principle of poetic tradition systematically to any poem or group of poems within the corpus of biblical Hebrew literature for the purpose of noting its significance as a literary-critical, that is to say, an interpretive, tool. The present monograph represents an initial attempt at filling this gap; "initial," because I am only too well aware of the insufficiency of what has here been done and of how much has yet to be done. But if these studies may for others serve as stimulus to further exploration and investigation the attempt will have been justified and the writer's efforts amply rewarded.

Because an aim of this work is the exposition of a specific element of biblical Hebrew poetic diction it would have been well, had it been possible, to select for study only those poems that are free of textual difficulty. But the texts on occasion exhibit questionable readings, and under such circumstances the major concern of the critic is, as it must be, the reconstruction of the "original" text. The difficulties encountered here take the form of scribal omissions, additions, and deliberate alterations. Fortunately, in the texts under investigation, many of the errors can be corrected with a reasonable degree of certainty. Nevertheless, the critic may not rule out the ever present possibility that what may appear as unintelligible to the modern reader may well have been perfectly intelligible to the ancient writer; while, on the other hand, apparent textual intelligibility can on occasion be shown to have been the result of later scribal activity. But in so far as poets have ever delighted in casting old materials in new forms, and new materials in old forms, the critic must be ever alive also to the possibility that the poet may have deliberately altered his manner in order to produce a new effect.

The Introduction is devoted to a discussion of general matters pertaining to parallelism and poetic tradition. Each of the following studies deals essentially with one particular poem or portions of a poem. These are among those generally classified as "early" and may be dated roughly to the pre-Solomonic period. The sequence of texts has been ordered not along chronological lines but along lines of increasing complexity; that is to say, the discussion proceeds from studies of the briefer (and therefore relatively more simple) to the longer (and therefore relatively more complex) poetic compositions.

At this point there is left but the very pleasant duty of singling out for thanks those to whom I feel a special indebtedness. Chief among these is H. L. Ginsberg and, only to a somewhat lesser degree, Umberto Cassuto and W. F. Albright. Those who are familiar with the pioneering comparative studies of these scholars will recognize on almost every page the enormity of my debt to them.

Only after the present work in all its essentials was completed, the evidence assembled, and the ideas formulated was I introduced to the theories of the late Professor Milman Parry, whose studies of the Homeric poems and other epic literature led him to recognize the importance, and to stress the significance, of tradition in the composition of ancient poetry. The literary traditions of Greek and Hebrew differ widely and fundamentally,[12] but to have learned that the force of tradition was as much a factor in early Greek as in Hebrew poetry and to have arrived independently at a similar explanation for such reliance upon it have helped strengthen my own convictions concerning the essential validity of the position reached.

To Professors Raymond A. Bowman, John A. Wilson, and, most particularly, I. J. Gelb, who graciously spared precious hours from demanding schedules to read the completed manuscript and to discuss several salient points and problems with me, I tender my warmest thanks.

With gratitude I acknowledge the financial aid rendered me by Emanuel Congregation of Chicago through the "Scholar in Residence" program established in memory of the late Albert Mecklenburger.

Lastly, I would acknowledge the encouragement of my friend Professor Geoffrey Hartman, who, during his brief stay here at the University of Chicago (the academic year 1960/1961) as Visiting Assistant Professor in the Department of English, accorded me the honor of attending several of my classes in biblical Hebrew poetry. In these classes I advanced the interpretations, theories, and evidence herein presented. Our discussions, in class and out, on general matters of literature and of literary criticism, have proved and doubtless will continue to prove an invaluable stimulus to my thinking. It was Dr. Hartman, too, who first drew my attention to the work of Milman Parry and who urged the formal publication of these studies.

In dedicating the fruit of these labors to my parents I but acknowledge in tiny measure the inspiration the memory of them ever affords.

S. G.

CHICAGO
October 1962

---

[12] Cf. Erich Auerbach, *Mimesis: The Representation of Reality in Western Literature* (trans. by W. Trask; New York, 1957) chap. i.

PREFACE TO SECOND EDITION

The invitation to authorize a reprint of this monograph allowed only for minor corrections and the inclusion of limited indices. To my student, Mr. Dennis G. Pardee, who assumed responsibility for the preparation of the latter, I am deeply obliged.

S. G.

LOS ANGELES, CALIFORNIA
March, 1973

INTRODUCTION

PARALLELISM AND TRADITION IN HEBREW POETRY

A GENERAL STATEMENT

N O POET'S work stands unique; it is no more *creatio ex nihilo,* an event
without precedent, than is its author without parentage. Every poet in his
day is but the last, the most recent, in a long line of poets from whose work he
may be said to have in some manner benefited and to whom, therefore, he is
indebted for an awareness of what may properly be called the essentials of his
craft. To fail to acknowledge these, to fail to recognize the inner logic in his
use of them, to fail to perceive the stylistic restrictions imposed upon him by
his poetic tradition, is to fail to grasp the formal foundations of his art, the
subtleties of his own particular genius, and the innumerable reverberations of
meaning that enhance the impact of his thought; in short, it is to ignore the distinctive qualities of his poetic achievement.

Of none is this more true, perhaps, than of the ancients, for whom, it would
appear, not the strikingly original but the meaningful manipulation of the
long-familiar constituted the apex of poetic technique. That this is unquestion-
ably true of the early Hebrews, and the nature and significance of their craft,
we hope in the subsequent chapters to demonstrate.

Biblical Hebrew poetic style, as generally conceived, is characterized by a
parallelism of thought and line. According to the common understanding,
parallelism in its simplest form is the relationship existing between two lines
in which the thought or construction of the first is echoed, positively or nega-
tively, in the second. The definition of Robert Lowth has never been super-
seded:

> The correspondence of one verse or line with another, I call parallelism. When a
> proposition is delivered, and a second is subjoined to it, or drawn under it, equivalent,
> or contrasted with it in sense, or similar to it in the form of grammatical construction,
> these I call parallel lines; and the words or phrases, answering one to another in the
> corresponding lines, parallel terms.[1]

In Lowth's, as in all subsequent general discussions of the subject, however,
emphasis has been placed on the correspondence in thought or sense between
the lines in parallel. The correspondence of the specific terms through which

[1] Lowth, *Isaiah,* p. ix.

that of thought or sense is made possible, if it has been the subject of discussion at all, has assumed an importance primarily in investigations of a lexicographical nature or has been schematized for the purpose of showing, in an abstract manner, which elements in the parallel lines correspond.[2] Yet it is apparent that parallelism of thought and line is possible necessarily and only by reason of the negative or positive correspondence in meaning of the terms which compose it.

Recognition of a virtually identical poetic style in the literature of ancient Ugarit generated, too, a recognition that the terms corresponding to one another in the parallel lines recurred in similar parallel relations elsewhere and frequently in both literatures. For example, in the Ugaritic text *UM* 127:55–57 occurs the following parallelism:[3]

יתֿבר חרנ ר אֹ שׁ -כֿ

עתֿתרת שמ בעל ק ד ק ד -כֿ

May (the deity) Ḥʀɴ break thy *head*,
(The deity) ᶜᴛᴛʀᴛ-Šᴍ-Bᶜʟ thy *pate!*

It is clear that the words to which attention is drawn by the separation of signs in the transliteration of the Ugaritic text and by italicization in the translation, "head" and "pate," correspond to one another and constitute what Lowth called in Hebrew poetry "parallel terms." When it is found that in a totally other context the same terms, in the same relationship, recur, for example *UM* 2 Aqht VI 36–37:

ספסנ יסכ]ל[-ר אֹ שׁ

חרצ לטֿר ק ד ק ד -י

Glaze will be poured on my *head*,
Plaster(?) on my *pate*,

or, again, *UM* 67 VI 14–16:

יצכ עמר אֹנ ל-ר אֹ שׁ -ה

עפר פלתֿת ל-ק ד ק ד -ה

He pours out dirt of mourning(?) on his *head*,
Dust of grieving on his *pate*,

the suspicion is aroused that the association of these terms in Ugaritic verse construction is the result not of chance but of design. Finding the same pair

---

[2] See particularly Louis I. Newman and William Popper, *Studies in Biblical Parallelism* Parts I and II ("Semicentennial Publications of the University of California" [1918]).

[3] Cf. Cassuto, *The Goddess Anath*, p. 25.

of terms in identical parallel relationship four times in Hebrew poetry,
Gen. 49:26:

תהיין ל- ר א ש יוסף

ול- ק ד ק ד נזיר אחיו

May they be on the *head* of Joseph,
And on the *pate* of the devoted one of his brothers,

Deut. 33:16:

תבואתה ל- ר א ש יוסף

ול- ק ד ק ד נזיר אחיו

May they come upon the *head* of Joseph,
And upon the *pate* of the devoted one of his brothers,

Ps. 7:17:

ישוב עמלו ב- ר א ש -ו

ועל ק ד ק ד -ו חמסו ירד

His villainy returns upon his *head*,
And upon his *pate* his violence descends,

Ps. 68:22:

אך אלהים ימחץ ר א ש איביו

ק ד ק ד שער מתהלך באשמיו

But God shall strike the *head* of his enemies,
The hairy(?) *pate* of the one who continues in his guilt,

helps confirm the suspicion of "design" and suggests that, having been employed not only in North Syria but in Palestine as well, the practice was related to, conditioned by, and dependent upon no geographical bounds but solely
literary traditional ones. The suspicion is further strengthened when it is found
that such pairs of parallel terms occurring in both Ugaritic and Hebrew
poetry number more than sixty. These form the foundation for the theory of a
traditional poetic diction common to Syro-Palestinian literatures.[4]

Since Hebrew poetry contains many more than these sixty-odd pairs of fixed
parallels and since extant Syro-Palestinian literature is limited, it follows that
if a pair of words found in parallel relationship in the Bible can be shown to
have been a fixed, or relatively fixed, pair for the Old Testament poets—even
if the pair has not yet made its appearance in Ugaritic or any other "Canaanite" literature—it must nevertheless represent an element of the same,
or a similar, literary tradition. This is the assumption upon which the present
work is founded.

[4] For lists of these pairs common to both Ugaritic and biblical Hebrew literature see particularly Cassuto, *The Goddess Anath*, pp. 24–28; Moshe Held, *Leshonenu* XVIII (1953)
144–60. In addition cf. A. Alt, *WO* I (1947–52) 283; S. Gevirtz, *JNES* XX (1961) 41–46.

From a modern perspective, conditioned by its prejudices of literary canons and taste, such fixed pairs are clichés. The charge is legitimate; but in the hands of a skilled poet, as we hope to show, the cliché can be transformed into an instrument of immense power and a most able vehicle for intense emotional expression. And once the principle of traditional diction be accepted, it can furthermore serve as a check on the integrity of the received text. These assertions can perhaps best be illustrated by a few examples.

In Ugaritic occurs the parallel pair כס // קבעת, "cup" // "goblet." The same pair is employed in Isaiah 51:17, 22.[5] A fixed pair, a cliché, as employed by the Ugaritic poet, *UM* 1 Aqht 215–16:

ינ] [כ ס בדי

ק ב ע ת בימני

(Take her and let her give me wine to drink)
[Let her place] the *cup* in my hand,
The *goblet* in my right hand,

when used by his Old Testament counterpart becomes

אשר שתית מיד יהוה את כ ו ס חמתו

את ק ב ע ת ... התרעלה שתית מצית

(Rouse thyself! rouse thyself! Get up Jerusalem!)
Thou who hast drunk from the hand of Yhwh the *cup* of his anger,
The *goblet* of reeling hast drunk to the dregs.

Again, the fixed pair נכר // זר, "strange(r)" // "foreign(er)," known thus far only in biblical poetry, occurs twelve times of a certainty and is clearly such another cliché,

Obad. 11:

ביום שבות ז ר י ם חִילו

ו- נ כ ר י ם באו שערו

On the day *strangers* carried off his substance,
And *foreigners* entered his gates,

Ps. 81:10:

לא יהיה בך אל ז ר

ולא תשתחוה לאל נ כ ר

There shall not be with thee a *strange* god,
Neither shalt thou bow down to a *foreign* god,

Prov. 27:2:

יהללך ז ר ולא פיך

נ כ ר י ואל שפתיך

[5] Cassuto, *The Goddess Anath*, p. 26.

Let a *stranger* praise thee, and not thine (own) mouth,
A *foreigner*, and not thine (own) lips,

and so on for nine additional occurrences.[6] When, in Ps. 69:9, we meet with

מוזר הייתי לאחי

ונכרי לבני אמי

the second term of the by now familiar parallel pair זר // נכר is readily noted, while the first appears separable from the otherwise unknown form מוזר. Accordingly, it becomes apparent that the text is to be emended and, in all probability, is to be read כ⟨מ⟩ו זר,[7] "like a stranger," so that the entire verse would read:

⟨כ⟩מו זר הייתי לאחי

ו-נכרי לבני אמי

Like a *stranger* have I become to my brothers,
And a *foreigner* to my mother's sons.

The fact that the second pair of parallel terms in this verse, אח(ים) // בנ(י) אם, "brother(s)" // "mother's son(s)," as we shall have occasion to demonstrate in a later chapter, is also a fixed pair, a cliché,[8] so that the entire verse with the exception of the verbal form is seen to have been composed of clichés, cannot detract from the poignancy and emotional power of the verse.

When we ask why poets, who were capable of the most original, profound, and moving thoughts world literature has ever known, should have had such regular and continual traffic with clichés, the answer must lie in an understanding of their dependence upon, and regard for, tradition. Reliance upon tradition, in turn, must find its *raison d'être* in some particular need to which it answered. This need, it may be suggested, had its genesis at a time when poetry was being composed without the aid of writing tools, that is to say, when poetic composition was an oral art. The poet had to construct his verses "on his feet," as it were, and to retain them in his memory. He was therefore forced to rely upon some mnemonic device, in this case upon a conventional diction and traditional patterns of composition. Syro-Palestinian poets, who formed their verses primarily in parallel lines, apparently found it expedient to employ conventionally fixed pairs of words. Such stylization enabled the poet more readily to compose and to retain his verses; for, once he had set forth a line of two, three, or four words or phrases, the formation of the parallel line

---

[6] Isa. 28:21; Prov. 2:16, 5:10 and 20, 7:5, 20:16, 27:13; Job 19:15; Lam. 5:2. Cf. also Isa. 61:5, Jer. 5:19, and, reading with the Septuagint, Prov. 23:27.

[7] Cf. *BH, ad loc.*

[8] Cf. Cassuto, *BASOR* No. 119 (1950) p. 18, n. 1.

was virtually at hand since the parallel terms, which would complete the thought, were already determined. The fixed pairs, therefore, constituted for the Syro-Palestinian poet what we have termed one of the "essentials of his craft." He doubtless acquired these through listening to the poems of his contemporaries and adapting for his own poetic needs those patterns of diction and verse structure that most pleased. New patterns could be, and were, formed; and as they conformed to the traditional modes of versification, and struck the poets' fancies as apt, would tend by repeated use to find their way into the repertory of poetic diction.

This phenomenon of dependence upon a traditional diction has recently been found to have obtained among the early Greeks as well. By careful analyses of epithets and phrases that find recurrent expression in the Homeric epics, the *Iliad* and the *Odyssey*, Professor Milman Parry was able to show conclusively what many had apparently suspected for some time, namely that such repetitions of stock expressions were not the result of accident, nor yet of an impoverished imagination, but of a long-established tradition.[9] So extensive in Homer's work did Parry find the use of such formulas, as he termed them, that the poems have come to be recognized by all subsequent students as having been composed almost entirely, if not entirely, of set phrases.

Parry similarly found the need for the reliance upon a fixed poetic diction in the limitations imposed upon the poets who composed their verses orally. Writing, he argued, permits a poet to leave his thought unfinished and sufficient leisure to search for, to find, and to alter new groupings of words with which to satisfy the requirements of his creation. In a society where writing is unknown, however, a poet is able to fashion his verses only if he has available to him a diction ready-made, a number of formulaic phrases at his command which he can easily arrange and rearrange to suit the specific needs of his poem's action.[10] The sources of these phrases, necessarily, are the poems of his predecessors and contemporaries which he has heard and whose poetic, if stock, phraseology he has mastered.

To the question of whether there was not to be found, in almost thirty thousand verses of Homer, a single "original" wording, Parry answered that the number of expressions that could not be shown to have been formulaic, or fashioned after the formulaic manner, was so infinitesimally small as to be reckoned insignificant and that the term "original" would have been for the early poets—as with reference to them—quite without meaning. It is clear,

[9] See particularly Parry's *L'Épithète traditionelle dans Homère* (Paris, 1928) and "Studies in the Epic Technique of Oral Verse-making" I and II, *HSCP* XLI (1930) 73–147 and XLIII (1932) 1–50. For a complete bibliography of Parry's work see *American Journal of Archaeology* LII (1948) 43 f.

[10] *HSCP* XLI 138 and XLIII 6.

therefore, as Parry has argued, that the ancient, pre-writing poet never sought to express anything new or in a new way; when faced with the necessity to do so, he formulated the idea in a manner as like that of his tradition as possible. These "creations," as Parry referred to them, would find acceptance, that is to say, were successful, only in so far as they accorded with the traditional, habitual practices of the poets and thus would themselves tend to become formulas.

Dependence upon formulaic phrases was further necessitated by the constraint upon the Greek poet to devise means whereby to express his thoughts in fixed meters. To answer this need, it has been found, not only the formulas but even individual words were, as a rule, restricted to one or, at most, two positions in the verse.[11] The formulas, then, served the additional, very specific and practical function of helping round out and perfect the metrical line.

Unlike the Greek, the Hebrew poet structured his verses not with whole formulaic phrases (though on occasion, as we shall indicate, this technique also was employed) but with fixed pairs of parallel terms. If these pairs were fitted into the lines in accordance with some principle of meter, it has yet to be discovered. That metrical considerations played a role is highly probable, but a demonstration of it—as clear as that for Greek verse—is not at hand.

Meter in Hebrew poetry has generally been described in terms of the number of stressed syllables. But meter, in the strict sense of the word, must account for unstressed syllables as well. Lowth's argument against the likelihood of defining the meters of biblical Hebrew poetry has never adequately been refuted: namely that the correct pronunciation of ancient Hebrew, the syllabification of many words, and the quantity and accent of the syllables are all highly uncertain.[12] Recourse to the sub- and supra-linear signs of the Massoretic text, the so-called "accents" or cantillation signs, for the purpose of determining accent is of questionable value. Two of these, whenever they occur, invariably appear on the first consonant of the word irrespective of the accent;[13] and four, whenever they occur, invariably appear on the final consonant of the word irrespective of the accent.[14] In addition, the fact of a Syro-Palestinian literary diction, common also to the biblical poets, with origins in remote antiquity, makes metrical schematizations as currently fashioned hazardous in the extreme. Ugaritic preserves case endings, while Hebrew, with rare exceptions according to the received text, does not. Since Hebrew does not preserve the case endings found in Ugaritic, while it does preserve the

---

[11] Cedric H. Whitman, *Homer and the Heroic Tradition* (Cambridge, Mass., 1958) pp. 109, 111.

[12] G. Gregory (trans.), *Lectures on the Sacred Poetry of the Hebrews*, p. 219; Lowth, *Isaiah*, pp. vii–viii. See also G. Douglas Young, "Ugaritic Prosody," *JNES* IX (1950) 124–33.

[13] *Yᵉṭîḇ, ṭᵉlîšāʾ gᵉḏôlā.*   [14] *Sᵉḡōltāʾ, pašṭāʾ, zarqāʾ, ṭᵉlîšāʾ qᵉṭannā.*

very specific word pairs, the meters would necessarily differ. It is merely a begging of the question to ignore all these difficulties and, in counting stresses alone (when even the exact placement of them is often uncertain!), to speak of meter. For what is counted most often is simply the number of words, or "significant" elements, in each colon.

The existence of meter, however, which we consider most probable, may account for some of the changes in tradition evident in Hebrew poetics. We may note, for example, the fixed pair of parallel terms חֻרץ // כסף, "silver" // "gold," occurring eighteen times in Ugaritic verse.[15] The same pair is found to have been employed in Hebrew poetry six times.[16] Far more frequent in Hebrew is the parallelism זהב // כסף, "silver" // "gold."[17] It is of interest to note that no biblical poet ever made use of the parallelism זהב // חרוץ, "gold₁" // "gold₂," from which we may perhaps infer (1) that tradition did not countenance this pair and (2) that the alteration in the regular parallelism, חרוץ // כסף to זהב // כסף, may perhaps have been dictated by metrical considerations. Of such matters, however, in our present state of knowledge, we can know nothing definite; but, if we may again employ the analogy of Greek epic diction, Parry has reasoned that

... when a change in the form of a word must also change its metrical value ... the poet, if he then wished to keep up with the spoken language, would have to put up with a phrase which was metrically false, or give it up altogether and make himself a new one.[18]

On the one hand, this explanation may account for the numerous archaisms preserved by Homer (i.e., archaic word forms retained for the sake of the meter) and, on the other, perhaps, for his "creations." Similarly in Hebrew, the retention of old—or importation of new—terms to form parallel pairs may have been motivated by the need to maintain metrical schemes. From the example cited above, חרוץ, in Hebrew, appears to have been the more archaic form, having cognates in Akkadian, Ugaritic, and Phoenician, while זהב has cognates in various Aramaic dialects and in Arabic.

A similar interpretation may perhaps explain the varied epithets employed as parallels to certain names. In Hebrew poetry we find the divine name Yʜᴡʜ paralleled by "the God of Israel," "the holy one of Israel," "the mighty one of Jacob," etc.; while in Ugaritic the divine name Bᶜʟ is paralleled by "the god Hᴅ," by "the son of Dɢɴ," by "the rider of the clouds," by ᶜʟʏ, and by

---

[15] *UM* 51 I 25–27, 27–28, 32–33, II 27–28, V 77–78, 94–95, 100–101, VI 34, 37–38; 77: 20–21; 124:14–15; 2 Aqht VI 17[–18]; Krt 126, 138, 205–6, [250–]251, 269–70, 282[–283].

[16] Zach. 9:3; Ps. 68:14; Prov. 3:14, 8:10, 8:19, 16:16.

[17] Isa. 13:17, 40:19, 46:6; Jer. 10:9; Hos. 2:10; Nah. 2:10; Zach. 13:9; Job 3:15, 28:1; Prov. 17:3, 27:21; Eccl. 12:6; Cant. 1:11, 3:10.

[18] *HSCP* XLIII 10.

"prince, lord of earth." Just as traditional epithets of certain characters in the Homeric epics were varied, as has been demonstrated, not to accord with the action being performed but solely with the requirements of meter,[19] so, very likely, were those in Syro-Palestinian verse. Until the metrical patterns of the latter are more closely defined, however, such explanations must be regarded as speculative.

Awareness of, and emphasis upon, the stylization of early verse, important as it is for an appreciation of the poets' craft, must not be permitted to obscure the uniqueness of the individual poem's vitality, which may be sought only in the imaginative utilization of tradition toward particular poetic ends. Again we may find instruction in the analogy of the Homeric epics. So heavy, to the modern student, seems the hand of tradition at work in these poems that it would appear to have stifled any poetic creativity. That this is not the case is evident from the power and appeal the *Iliad* and the *Odyssey* have ever exerted. The creativity of the poet clearly, therefore, must lie elsewhere than in his subject matter or in his diction, both of which, by scholarly consensus, were his by inheritance and not by invention. As a recent critic has written,

> There is no evidence at all that the poet of the *Iliad* invented a single character or episode in his whole poem. He may not even have invented a single phrase. His invention was the *Iliad*.[20]

So too the creativity of the Hebrew poet will not be found by the application of any modern requirement for "originality." Rather is it in the reworking of old themes by means of conventional phraseology, in traditional manner, to reproduce familiar actions uniquely and poetically significant that the poet's genius is to be sought. Since his tradition, for the most part, demanded the construction of verses in parallel cola by means of traditionally fixed word-pairs, it is in the poet's arrangement of these with one another, his ability in so doing to give to the lines composed of the conventionally correspondent terms distinctive meaning, and his harmonious setting of these in a larger whole—fashioning thereby a unity, with part answering to part—that the impact of his poem's force will have been felt. Clearly, the more skillful or gifted the poet, the more intense the emotional response of his audience and the greater its appreciation.

Such dissection of the poems' parts and elucidation of tradition as we propose to undertake in the following studies cannot diminish appreciation of the poetry, for we aim at isolating the distinctive qualities of the individual use of tradition and, as occasion may permit, clarifying the hidden and the obscure.

---

[19] Parry, *L'Épithète traditionelle dans Homère*. But cf. Seth Benardete, "Achilles and Hector: The Homeric Hero" (Unpublished Ph.D. dissertation, Committee on Social Thought, University of Chicago, 1955) pp. 71 f., who argues that "Homer manages [the] use [of epithet] more finely than many suppose."

[20] Whitman, *Homer and the Heroic Tradition*, p. 14.

STUDY I

THE WOMEN'S EULOGY OF SAUL AND DAVID[1]

FOLLOWING a successful military campaign against the Philistines, the returning Israelite warriors were met by their women-folk, who came out of the cities dancing and playing on instruments while chanting the following lyric in praise of the commanders, Saul and David:

הכה שאול באלפו
ודוד ברבבתיו

Saul hath smitten his thousands,
And David his ten-thousands.

This activity of women, hailing returning victors with music and dancing, appears to have been traditional in early Israel. We are told, for example, that Miriam led the women in song and dance when the pursuing Egyptian host had been vanquished (Exod. 15:20), and, after Jephthah's victory over the Ammonites, his daughter, similarly, is said to have come out to greet him with music and dancing (Judg. 11:34). Furthermore, as late as the nineteenth century, a like practice has been observed among Bedouin women who welcomed their tribe's returning fighters with song and dance.[2]

The exuberant praise thus heaped upon the two war-leaders, Saul and David, has been turned into something quite other than that by the interpretation the author of the narrative has placed upon it (I Sam. 18:8):

And Saul became very angry, and this thing was evil in his eyes, and he said, "They have given to David ten-thousands, and to me have they given the thousands. And what is there left for him but the kingdom?"

Most modern scholars, following the biblical historian's lead, have seen in the simple praise-song of the women an indication of the growing popularity of the younger man at the expense of the dwindling reputation of the older. There has thus been imputed to the women's eulogy a kind of invidious comparison between the two men, reason enough for Saul's ensuing jealousy. That the author of the prose account intended this interpretation is clear; writing not only after the event in question but doubtless also long after the fall of the house of Saul and the establishment of the house of David and seeking causes

[1] Sam. 18:7.

[2] Charles M. Doughty, *Travels in Arabia Deserta* I (Cambridge, 1888) 452.

15

to explain the rift that occurred between the two, he has utilized this bit of folk poetry as evidence. Whether the women who chanted the song intended the comparison, or, perhaps better, whether the poem itself actually contains reference to superior ability on the part of David, I believe a more critical examination of it would show to be doubtful.

We may note in the couplet two distinct sets of parallel terms: that of the names, "Saul" // "David," and that of the numbers, "thousands" // "ten-thousands." The latter is a fixed pair. In addition to its occurrence here and in the two quotations of this text (I Sam. 21:12 and 29:5), it is found elsewhere in Old Testament poetry, for example in Hebrew,

Deut. 32:30:

איכה ירדף אחד א ל ף

ושנים יניסו ר ב ב ה

How might one chase away a *thousand*,
Or two cause *ten-thousand* to flee?

Mic. 6:7:

הירצה יהוה ב- א ל פ י אילים

ב- ר ב ב ו ת נחלי שמן

Shall Yhwh be pleased with *thousands* of rams,
With *ten-thousands* of wadis of oil?

Ps. 91:7:

יפל מצדך³ א ל ף

ו- ר ב ב ה מימינך

There shall fall at thy side³ a *thousand*,
And *ten-thousand* at thy right hand,

etc.,[4] and in Aramaic, Dan. 7:10:

א ל ף א ל פ י ם ישמשונה

ו- ר ב ו ר ב ו ן קדמוהי יקומון

A *thousand thousands* served him,
And *ten-thousand ten-thousands* stood before him.

Moreover, the pair is very frequently employed in Ugaritic,

UM 51 I 27–29:[5]

יצק כספ ל- א ל פ מ

חֿרצ יצקמ ל- ר ב ב ת

³ Cassuto has emended the text to read מִידְךָ, probably rightly, on the basis of the fixed parallelism ימין // יד, "hand" // "right hand," occurring both in Ugaritic and in Hebrew verse; see *The Goddess Anath*, p. 25.

[4] Cf. also Deut. 33:17 and perhaps Gen. 24:60 and Ps. 68:18 as well.

[5] Cf. *UM* 77:20–21.

He smelts silver by the *thousands*,
Gold he smelts by the *ten-thousands*,

UM 51 V 86:[6]

ב- אָ ל פ שׁד

ר ב ת כמנ

Over the *thousand* fields,
Ten-thousand lots,

UM 51 V 118–19:

אָ ל פ שׁד אָחֹד בת

ר ב ת כמנ הכל

A *thousand* fields shall the house o'erspread,
Ten-thousand lots the palace,

UM Krt 92–93:[7]

הלכ ל-אָ ל פ מ הֹסֹ

ול- ר ב ת כמיר

They proceed by *thousands* . . .
And by *ten-thousands* . . . ,

UM ꜥnt I 15–17:

אָ ל פ כד יקח בחֹמר

ר ב ת ימסכ במסכה

A *thousand* jugs of wine doth he take,
Ten-thousand doth he mix in his mixture,

PRU II, No. 19:4–5:

תעזזכ אָ ל פ ימם

ו-ר ב ת שנת

May (the gods) strengthen thee a *thousand* days,
Even *ten-thousand* years.

That the terms "thousand" // "ten-thousand" constituted, as may be seen, a fixed pair, a cliché, might itself cast suspicion on any comparison intended in the praise-song. This is increased on investigation of the manner and significance of the poetic use of numerals generally in biblical verse.[8]

[6] Cf. *UM* 51 VIII 24–26, 2 Aqht V 9–10, ꜥnt IV 82, ꜥnt Pl. vi VI 17–18.

[7] Cf. *UM* Krt 180–81.

[8] A little more than a year after the present study had been completed and shortly before the entire manuscript had been submitted for publication, there appeared an article by Wolfgang M. W. Roth entitled "The Numerical Sequence x/x + 1 in the Old Testament," *VT* XII (1962) 300–311. Because certain references to primary and secondary sources (one of which I consider to be the true explanation of number parallelism) have been overlooked by Dr. Roth and because I have arrived at a vastly different conclusion regarding the meaning of the verse, despite the essentially similar assemblage of data in our two studies, I have thought it best to leave this portion of the work entirely unchanged, particularly since the

The curious parallelism of numbers which employs two different numerals as correspondent terms, as far as I have been able to learn, was first observed by Robert Lowth, who found it "a peculiar figure . . . altogether poetical." Lowth regarded it as the use of a definite number for an indefinite and utilized chiefly for the sake of the parallelism, since, as he noted, ". . . the circumstances afterwards enumerated do not accord with the number specified."[9] Subsequent investigators, similarly, found "ascending numeration" to be a rhetorical device employed to express an indefinite (significant or insignificant) number or total,[10] or a general numeration without concern for arithmetic precision, indicating merely that the roster of things assembled is incomplete,[11] and similar descriptions.[12] Only Ginsberg seems to have proceeded beyond such banal interpretation of the phenomenon to suggest as the principle underlying such constructions the requirements of "a parallelism of equivalents."[13] In the absence of synonymous terms for specific numbers, what he termed "graded numerals" were substituted.

As employed by the biblical poets, the general pattern of numbers (whether cardinal or ordinal) of one-digit magnitude in parallel relationship is "*x*" // "*x* + 1," for example

Ps. 62:12:

אחת דבר אלהים

שתים זו שמעתי

Once hath God spoken,
Twice have I heard this,

Job 33:14:[14]

כי ב-אחת ידבר אל

וב-שתים לא ישורנה

For God speaketh in *one* way,
And in *two* though (man) doth not perceive it,

---

interpretation of the text in the study immediately following is dependent, in large part, on the understanding gained in this. In n. 21 (p. 21) I have called attention to those sources included in Roth's study that have been overlooked in this.

[9] G. Gregory (trans.), *Lectures on the Sacred Poetry of the Hebrews*, p. 218.

[10] GKC, § 134 *s*.

[11] Crawford H. Toy, *A Critical and Exegetical Commentary on the Book of Proverbs* ("International Critical Commentary" [Edinburgh, 1899]) pp. 127 f.

[12] S. R. Driver and G. B. Gray, *A Critical and Exegetical Commentary on the Book of Job* I ("International Critical Commentary" [New York, 1921]) 55 f.; *UM*, § 7.7; etc.

[13] H. L. Ginsberg, *The Legend of King Keret* ("*BASOR* Supplementary Studies," Nos. 2–3 [New Haven, Conn., 1946]) pp. 40 f.

[14] Cf. Deut. 32:30, Jer. 3:14, Job 40:5, Ecclesiasticus 50:25; the Greek version of the last book (25:7) preserves a parallelism of 9 // 10.

Amos 1:3:[15]

על ש ל ש ה פשעי דמשק

ועל א ר ב ע ה לא אשיבנו

For *three* transgressions of Damascus,
And for *four* I will not restore it,

Prov. 30:15:[16]

ש ל ו ש הנה לא תשבענה

א ר ב ע לא אמרו הון

Three things are never satisfied,
Four never say, "Enough,"

Prov. 6:16:

ש ש הנה שנא יהוה

ו- ש ב ע תועבות נפשו

Six things doth Yнwн hate,
And *seven* are his disgust,

Job 5:19:

ב- ש ש צרות יצילך

וב- ש ב ע לא יגע בך רע

From *six* troubles shall he deliver thee,
And in *seven* shall no evil touch thee,

Mic. 5:4:

והקמנו עליו ש ב ע ה רעים

ו- ש מ נ ה נסיכי אדם

And we shall raise against him *seven* shepherds,
And *eight* leaders of man,

Eccl. 11:2:

תן חלק ל- ש ב ע ה

וגם ל- ש מ ו נ ה

Give a portion to *seven*,
And also to *eight*.

The same principle of number parallelism is found to have been employed by the Ugaritic poets. As examples we may cite

UM 51 III 17–18:

ת̄ נ דבחם שנא̄ בעל

ת̄ ל ת̄ רכב ערפת

Two (kinds of) sacrifices doth Baal hate,
Three, the Rider of the Clouds,

[15] Cf. Amos 1:6, 9, 11, 13 and 2:1, 4, 6.
[16] Cf. Prov. 30:18, 21, 29.

UM Krt 205–6:[17]

תֵ נ ה כ(!)ספפם אָתֵן

ו-תֵ ל תֵ תֵ ה חרצמ

Twice her (. . .) (in) silver will I give,
Thrice her (. . .) (in) gold,

UM 125:84–85:

תֵ ל תֵ ירחֵם כמו[רצ]

אֵ ר ב ע כדו כו[רת]

Three months hath he been s[ick],
Four hath K[rt] been ill,

UM Krt 83–84:[18]

יאֵף לחם ד-חֵ מ ש

מעֵד תֵ ד תֵ ירחֵם

Let bread be baked for a *fifth*,
Food for a *sixth* month,

UM 1 Aqht 42–44:

ש ב ע שנת יצרכ בעל

תֵ מ נ רכב ערפת

Seven years may Baal fail,
Eight, the Rider of the Clouds,

UM Krt 8–9:[19]

ד-ש ב ע [אֵ]חֵם לה

תֵ מ נ ת בנ אֵם

Who had *seven* [bro]thers,
Eight mother's sons.

Aramaic literature also evidences this pattern of number parallelism, for example Aḥiqar, col. vi 92:

תר תין מלן שפירה

וזי תל תא רחימה לשמש

Two things are pleasing,
And a *third* beloved by (the god) Šmš,[20]

---

[17] Cf. *UM* ꜥnt IV 79–80 and 3 Aqht 22–23, 33–34.

[18] Cf. *UM* Krt 174–75.

[19] Cf. *UM* 52:66–67, 67 V 8–9, 75 II 45–46, 128 II 23–24, ꜥnt V 19 and 34–35.

[20] Cf. the remarks of Ginsberg, *ZAW* LV (1937) 309. The parallelism 7 // 8 appears in an Aramaic incantation text; see James A. Montgomery, *Aramaic Incantation Texts from Nippur* (Philadelphia, 1913) pp. 105, 195–200. Cf. Albright, *BASOR* No. 76 (1939) p. 9, n. 28.

as does Akkadian in rare examples thus far limited to incantation literature,
Maqlû VI 121–22:

> *šá a-na* I KASKAL.GID-*àm ip-pu-ḫu* IZI
> *a-na* II KASKAL.GID *iš-tap-pa-ra* DUMU *šip-ri-šá*
>
> Who, for *one* double-hour has kindled fire,
> For *two* double-hours has sent her messenger,

Maqlû III 31–32:

> II-*ta ši-na* DUMU.SAL.MEŠ ᵈ*A-nim šá* AN-*e*
> III-*ta ši-na* DUMU.SAL.MEŠ ᵈ*A-nim šá* AN-*e*
>
> *Two* are they, the daughters of (the god) Anu of heaven,
> *Three* are they, the daughters of (the god) Anu of heaven,

Maqlû IV 109:[21]

> VI KEŠDA-*ši-na* // VII *pit-ru-ú-a*
>
> *Six* are their bindings,
> *Seven*, my loosenings.

Parallelism of two-digit numbers is found to have been schematized according to the patterns "10 x" // "10 $(x + 1)$" and "10 $x + x$" // "10 $(x + 1) + x + 1$," where "x" is a one-digit numeral. Hebrew provides only one example of this pattern, "The days of our years are *seventy* years, or even by reason of strength *eighty* years" (Ps. 90:10), but it is well attested in Ugaritic,[22]

UM 128 IV 6–7:

> תֹרי [מ]ע ב ש ח צ
> יי[בֹ]ט מ נ י ם תֹ
>
> Invite my *seven*[*ty*] "bulls,"
> My *eighty* "[gazel]les,"

UM 51 VII 11–12:

> [.. מ]ל בעל מ נ י ם תֹ
> [.. מר]ל בעל מ ע ש ת
>
> *Eighty* Baal [. . .],
> *Ninety* Baal [. . .],

UM 51 VII 9–10:

> ער אַחד מ תֹ תֹ-ל תֹ תֹ
> פדר ע [!ב ש מ ע ב ש

---

[21] W. G. Lambert *apud* Roth, *VT* XII 304 and n. 4, drew attention to the parallelism 6 // 7 in an incantation text published by J. J. A. van Dijk, *Sumer* XIII (1957) 93–95. Roth has further noted the parallelism of the numbers 2 // 3 in a Sumerian text translated by S. N. Kramer, *From the Tablets of Sumer* (Indian Hills, Col., 1956) p. 144.

[22] It has been noted also in a Hittite epical text; see *Orientalistische Literaturzeitung* XL (1937) 518, n. 1. Cf. also Roth, *VT* XII 307, n. 2.

Sixty-six towns he seized,
Seventy-seven villages,

UM 67 V 19–21:[23]

שכב עמנה שבע ל-שבעם
[...] לי תמנ ל-תמנים

He lay with her *seventy-seven* times,
[. . .] *eighty-eight* times,

and in Akkadian, again in a rare example, Gilgamesh XI 300–301:

ana XX [KASKAL.GÍD] *ik-su-pu ku-sa-pa*
ana XXX KASKAL.GÍD *iš-ku-nu nu-bat-ta*

At *twenty* [double-hours] they broke off a morsel,
At *thirty* double-hours they settled for the night.

From the foregoing it appears evident that the traditional mode of utilizing numbers in parallel lines demanded a gradation such that the number in the first of the corresponding lines was matched or corrected[24] by a number of the next higher unit in the following line. One-digit numbers had as their fixed parallels the next higher one-digit number (1 // 2, 2 // 3, 3 // 4, 5 // 6, 6 // 7, 7 // 8); two-digit numbers had as their fixed parallels the corresponding next higher two-figure unit (20 // 30, 70 // 80, 80 // 90, 66 // 77, 77 // 88). The only all-inclusive explanation of this phenomenon would appear to be that the pattern of "ascending numeration" itself was as much a fixed tradition as any other set of traditionally parallel terms. It is futile, therefore, to argue the definite or indefinite status of any pair of numerals outside the specific context of a particular poem or to speculate on the significance of the consistency or inconsistency of numbers and things enumerated. Once the poet had selected a number to be used in parallelism, its correspondent was already determined.

In the poem under discussion, the numbers in parallel are "thousands" // "ten-thousands." We have already noted that these two numbers as used in Hebrew, Aramaic, and Ugaritic verse compose a fixed pair. As such, they must follow the very same pattern as that governing other pairs of numbers, thereby implying that "ten-thousand" is simply the corresponding and next higher unit after "thousand." That, poetically, *ten-thousand* followed as the sequent of *thousand* is most clearly demonstrated in Deut. 32:30:

איכה ירדף אחד אלף
ו-שנים יניסו רבבה

How might *one* chase away a *thousand,*
Or *two* cause *ten-thousand* to flee?

---

[23] Cf. *UM* 75 II 49–50.
[24] Cf. Ginsberg, *The Legend of King Keret,* pp. 40 f.

Here we note in the parallel lines two fixed pairs of numbers: "one" // "two" and "thousand" // "ten-thousand." Were *ten-thousand* not simply the next higher unit after *thousand*, a fixed parallel of it, it might legitimately be expected that the ratio of *one* to *two* would apply to the second set of numbers and that *thousand* would have *two-thousand* as its correspondent term in this particular verse. That it has instead *ten-thousand*, the fixed corresponding term, without regard for mathematical consistency, seems to argue conclusively for the operation of a poetic tradition in which *thousand* is to *ten-thousand* as *one* is to *two*. That is to say, just as *two* is the next higher unit after *one*, so *ten-thousand* is the next higher unit after *thousand*—not in any mathematical but in the poetical scheme.

One other element may be introduced at this point in support of our thesis that the significance of the praise-song is to be understood from a literary-traditional perspective rather than from any other and that the author of the prose account—not of the song—is responsible for the interpretation of it as containing a comparison of Saul and David to the detriment of Saul. The additional bit of evidence is the remark attributed to Saul immediately following the chant, I Sam. 18:8:

נתנו לדוד ר ב ב ו ת

ולי נתנו ה-א ל פ י ם

They have given to David *ten-thousands*,
And to me have they given the *thousands*.

Though not apparently poetic, this statement utilizes a poetic device: the reversal of the order of parallel terms. In Study III we shall have occasion to discuss in greater detail alteration of traditionally fixed pairs by Syro-Palestinian poets; for the present it may suffice to draw the reader's attention to our remarks elsewhere[25] which indicate that one of the explanations for reversal in the sequence of a fixed parallel pair was the employment of the same pair in traditional sequence immediately before. This situation obtains here and would seem to indicate that the author of the prose narrative was fully cognizant of poetic technique, employing an aspect of it here himself.

In addition, his use of the definite article (which many modern scholars would unjustly correct) may perhaps represent still another aspect of this tradition, since its appearance with one element of a pair of fixed parallel terms, to the exclusion of the other, is found elsewhere in Old Testament poetry, for example Ps. 114:6:

ה - הרים תרקדו כאילים

גבעות כבני צאן

---

[25] *JNES* XX 46 and n. 9.

> *The* mountains skipped like rams,
> Hills like the young of the flock.

The implication that most would locate in the women's eulogy, therefore, that David's military prowess was being lauded over that of Saul's, appears poorly founded. And is it not furthermore incredible that the welcoming party of women—singing and dancing, obviously pleased and proud of the accomplishment of their men—should be thought to have seized just this opportunity, his return from victory, to insult their king? The song contains no insult. It is a lavish praise of both Saul and David, utilizing the largest (single) equivalent numerals available in Syro-Palestinian poetic diction: the fixed pair "thousands" // "ten-thousands."[26] Had they really intended to exaggerate the feats of David beyond those of Saul, poetic means to do so were at their disposal, as we hope to demonstrate in Study II.

[26] Roth, *VT* XII 303, has correctly and astutely pointed out that, except for the verse under consideration, all the examples of number parallelism in Hebrew verse (he might have added Ugaritic as well) exhibit either synonymous or synthetic parallelism. Yet it does not seem sufficiently to have impressed him that, were the significance of the song truly "the exaltation of David over Saul," this would be the sole instance in all Ugaritic and Hebrew verse of the use of numbers in an antithetic parallelism.

STUDY II

LAMECH'S SONG TO HIS WIVES[1]

עדה וצלה שמען קולי
נשי למך האזנה אמרתי

כי איש הרגתי לפצעי
וילד לחברתי

כי שבעתים יקם קין
ולמך שבעים ושבעה

Adah and Zillah hear my voice!
Wives of Lamech give ear to my speech!

Because I have slain a man for my wound,
Even a boy for my hurt.

If Cain be avenged sevenfold,
Then Lamech seventy and seven!

THE song expresses Lamech's overweening pride, his refusal to suffer any hurt without a severalfold and dire revenge. This expression of arrogant self-conceit and disdain for customary retribution is skillfully reinforced by the poet through a clever manipulation of poetic convention. Following the initial couplet, each of whose three component pairs of parallel terms has been structured entirely in accordance with the Syro-Palestinian poetic tradition, there ensues a rapid and continued disintegration of the tradition of fixed pairs, climaxed in the final couplet with the hero's exaggerated and pretentious claim, which the poet has fashioned by the formulation of a deliberately non-traditional and even outlandish parallelism.

Its age cannot be determined with any certainty, but "the fierce implacable spirit of revenge that forms the chief part of the Bedouin's code of honour"[2] and animates the present poem accentuates its primitive quality, and most scholars concur in assigning it a high antiquity. Study of the names of the hero and his wives lends a measure of support to this conclusion. While the women's names, עדה and צלה, are attested in late periods, they are also found as ele-

---

[1] Gen. 4:23–24.

[2] John Skinner, *A Critical and Exegetical Commentary on Genesis* ("International Critical Commentary" [2d ed.; Edinburgh, 1930]) p. 120.

ments of longer proper names in the Old Akkadian period, with צלה being particularly common.³ The name למך, it may be suggested, is to be identified with
the Old Akkadian names *Lam-ki-um* and *Lam-kiₓ-Ma-ri*.⁴ If the latter identi-
fication prove correct, then outside the biblical references to this particular
individual the only occurrences of this name or name element, למך, are these of
the earliest period for which Semitic names are attested.

Beginning his song in conventional manner, the hero addresses his wives:

עדה וצלה שמען קולי
נשי למך האזנה אמרתי

Adah and Zillah hear my voice!
Wives of Lamech give ear to my speech!

Three sets of parallel terms may be distinguished: "Adah and Zillah" //
"wives of Lamech," "hear" // "give ear," and "voice" // "speech." Though
the first of these, "Adah and Zillah" // "wives of Lamech," does not recur, it
may nevertheless be regarded as having been constructed according to the
manner of the Syro-Palestinian poets, for the setting of a noun or proper name
in parallel formation with a descriptive or identifying word or epithet was a
pattern, a regular feature of their style. We cite but one example from Ugaritic
and one from Hebrew verse,

UM Krt 135–36:⁵

אֻדְם יתנתׁ אׁ ל

וׁאׁשׁנ אׁ בׁ אׁ דׁ מ

ʾUdm is a gift of ʾIl,
And a present of the *father of Man*,

Judg. 5:7:

עַד שקמתי דׁ בׁ וׁ רׁ ה

שקמתי אׁ ם בׁ יׁ שׁ רׁ אׁ ל

Until thou didst arise *Deborah*,
Didst arise a *mother in Israel.*

To this very frequently appearing parallel construction may perhaps be applied the designation "epithetic" parallelism,⁶ other examples of which will be
found below in Study IV.

³ Cf. I. J. Gelb, *Glossary of Old Akkadian* (*MAD* No. 3 [1957]) pp. 16 (under "Ur III
PN's") and 243 f. respectively.

⁴ For references see *ibid.* p. 162 (under "LMG?"). On the value *kiₓ* (Gelb: *ki₄*) for ɢɪ₄ in
Old Akkadian writing, see Gelb, *Old Akkadian Grammar and Writing* (*MAD* No. 2 [2d ed.;
1961]) p. 90, No. 176, who cites the spelling *wa-ar-gi₄-um*.

⁵ Cf. *UM* Krt 277 f.

⁶ To specify this type of parallelism in Sumerian poetry the term "particularizing" has
been employed by Thorkild Jacobsen, *JNES* XII (1953) 162, n. 5.

That the verbs "hear" // "give ear" constituted a fixed pair in Hebrew poetry may be inferred from the pair's sixteen additional occurrences in biblical verse with the verbs in this sequence[7] and two with the verbs in reverse sequence,[8] for example

Judg. 5:3:

שמעו מלכים

האזינו רזנים

Hear, O kings!
Give ear, O rulers!

Isa. 1:2:

שמעו שמים

ו-האזיני ארץ

Hear, O heavens!
And *give ear*, O earth!

Ps. 54:4:

אלהים שמע תפלתי

האזינה לאמרי פי

O God, *hear* my prayer!
Give ear to the words of my mouth!

The pair "voice" // "speech" may be noted again in

Isa. 28:23:

האזינו ושמעו קולי

הקשיבו ושמעו אמרתי

Give ear and hear my *voice!*
Attend and hear my *speech!*

Isa. 29:4*b:*

והיה כאוב מארץ קולך

ומעפר אמרתך תצפצף

And thy *voice* shall be like a ghost from the earth,
And from the dust thy *speech* shall resound,

Isa. 32:9:[9]

נשים שאננות קמנה שמענה קולי

בנות בטחות האזנה אמרתי

O carefree women arise (and) hear my *voice!*
Trusting daughters give ear to my *speech!*

[7] Num. 23:18; Judg. 5:3; Isa. 1:2 and 10, 32:9; Hos. 5:1; Joel 1:2; Ps. 17:1, 39:13, 49:2, 54:4, 84:9, 143:1; Job 33:1, 34:2 and 16. Cf. also Exod. 15:26 and Deut. 1:45.

[8] Deut. 32:1, Isa. 42:23; cf. also Isa. 28:23.

[9] In addition cf. Ps. 5:2–3 and perhaps also Ps. 19:4 and Prov. 1:20–21.

With the succeeding bi-colon the poet begins the deliberate breakdown of his tradition. The rejection is not thoroughgoing, for the couplet is composed of two seeming pairs of parallel terms; but the first is odd and not otherwise known, while the second can hardly be construed as a particularly poetic parallelism:

כי איש הרגתי לפצעי
וילד לחברתי

Because I have slain a man for my wound,
Even a boy for my hurt.

The parallelism of איש, "man," or, as it might better be rendered, "some-one,"[10] with ילד, "boy," occurs only here and is curious on two counts. Firstly, the regular parallel of איש, "man," in Old Testament verse is בן אדם, "son of Man," as may be seen from its several occurrences,[11] for example

Num. 23:19:

לא א י ש אל ויכזב
ו- ב ן א ד ם ויתנחם

God is not a *man* that he should lie,
Or a *son of Man* that he should repent,

Prov. 8:4:

אליכם א י ש י ם אקרא
וקולי אל ב נ י א ד ם

Unto you, O *men*, do I call,
And my voice (is) unto the *sons of Man*,

Job 35:8:

ל-א י ש כמוך רשעך
ול-ב ן א ד ם צדקתך

Thy wickedness concerns a *man* as thyself,
And thy righteousness a *son of Man*.

Secondly, it must surely strike the reader as odd that the poet should deliber-ately have elected to employ the term "boy," that he should have his hero boast of having slain a mere boy (for discussion of significance of this term in its present context see pp. 30–34).

The terms composing the remaining parallelism of the couplet, "wound" //

[10] I.e., as an indefinite pronoun, a meaning it very often bears; cf. Gen. 10:5, Exod. 25:20, Isa. 36:18 (=II Kings 18:33), Job 41:9 and 43:11, etc. For discussion see I. Eitan, *AJSL* XLIV (1928) 190.

[11] Num. 23:19; Isa. 52:14; Jer. 49:18 and 33, 50:40, 51:43; Mic. 5:6; Ps. 80:18; Prov. 8:4; Job 35:8; and, in prose, I Kings 8:39 (=II Chron. 6:30). In reverse sequence: Jer. 32:19; Ps. 49:3, 62:10. Cf. also Isa. 51:12, 56:2; Ps. 8:5, 90:3; Job 16:21, 25:6.

"hurt," are found associated elsewhere in biblical literature but not again in poetic parallelism. For example they occur as the last in the series of propositions comprising the so-called "Law of Talion," Exod. 21:23–25:

If any harm follow then thou shalt give life for life, eye for eye, tooth for tooth, hand for hand, foot for foot, burn for burn, *wound* (פצע) for *wound* (פצע), *hurt* (חבורה) for *hurt* (חבורה),

in Isa. 1:6:

מכף רגל ועד ראש אין בו מתם

פ צ ע ו-ח ב ו ר ה ומכה טריה

From the sole of the foot even unto the head there is no soundness in it:
(But) *wound*(s) and *hurt*(s) and raw bruise(s),

and in Prov. 20:30:

ח ב ר ו ת פ צ ע תמריק ברע

ומכות חדרי בטן

Hurts of a *wound* cleanse (one) from evil,
And bruises (cleanse one's) inner recesses.

With the final couplet the disintegration of the tradition of fixed pairs of parallel terms is complete:

כי שבעתים יקם קין

ולמך שבעים ושבעה

If Cain be avenged sevenfold,
Then Lamech seventy and seven!

The reference here is to Lamech's ancestor, the first-born son of Adam and Eve, who, having slain his brother, was exiled by God. Fearful of his life, Cain had appealed to God and had been granted the protection of a sevenfold revenge. Lamech vaunts himself even beyond his infamous forebear, and his exaggeration is underscored by the very composition of his pretentious bravado. The parallelism in which this may be seen and which commands our attention is that of the numbers "sevenfold" // "seventy and seven." We have already noted in the preceding study the tradition of number parallelism so common in Syro-Palestinian verse, a tradition which required a gradation of numerals in successive lines such that the figure employed in the second of two parallel lines was one unit larger than that in the first. The significance of this pattern, it was stressed, lay in the "equivalence" of the two numbers. Had the present couplet, therefore, been fashioned after this pattern of Syro-Palestinian number parallelism the sequent of "sevenfold" would of necessity have been "eightfold," or, conversely, the correspondent of "seventy and seven" appearing in the second colon would have had to be "sixty and six" in the first colon. But, had either of these parallelisms been employed, Lamech's meaning would have been that his claim to revenge was as great as that of Cain. And this is the point of the poem and of its nontraditional final couplet: Lamech pretends to an even greater—an exaggerated—measure of revenge and is made to do so through a disproportionate parallelism of numbers.

ADDITIONAL NOTE ON ילד, "BOY," IN THE PARALLELISM איש // ילד

Modern scholars are generally agreed that the lines

> For I have slain a *man* for my wound,
> Even a *boy* for my hurt,

constitute a synonymous parallelism and that the parallel terms "man" // "boy," therefore, have reference to one and the same individual. The difficulties here, as we have indicated, are two: (1) the parallelism "man" // "boy" is a deliberate rejection of the traditional "man" // "son of Man" parallelism, and (2) the question inevitably arises, why should Lamech boast of having slain a boy, a child?[12] What is eminently clear is that the poet, having deliberately rejected the regular parallel "son of Man," as well as such terms to denote a grown man as אדם, גבר, אנוש, or even בחור, has selected the term "boy" with care—and means precisely what he says. His opponent, his adversary, the object of his act of violence was a boy.

Now there is reason to believe that warriors and, more particularly, war-leaders and heroes in the ancient world were considerably younger than we are wont to imagine. Admittedly, evidence for this belief is largely circumstantial, but enough exists to warrant the assertion.

Among the military figures of classical antiquity about whom clear and relevant evidence is available may be cited Alexander the Great, who, though of scholarly bent and reluctant to follow the military career of his father, was nevertheless in command of the cavalry at the Battle of Chaeronea at the age of eighteen. At nineteen, after his father died, Alexander reconquered all Macedonia and Greece and at twenty invaded Asia. And Hannibal, it is known, was being trained in the art of war at least as early as his ninth year.

From cuneiform sources we learn that Yasmaḫ-Addu, set upon the throne of Mari by his conqueror father, Shamshi-Addu, was evidently very young and hardly, perhaps, out of childhood.[13] Yet the father berates the boy for

---

[12] The Revised Standard Version's translation of the word here as "young man" only serves to hide, not to solve, the problem.

[13] His father refers to him as being a child, e.g. in *ARM* I 85:6: *ù at-ta ṣi-iḫ-re-ta*, "And thou, thou art a child." It may also be worthy of note that Shamshi-Addu arranges a mar-

failing to emulate his older brother who "has made a great name" for himself gaining military victories. Despite his extreme youth, Yasmaḫ-Addu was expected to "act the man" and lead his troops in military expeditions.[14]

In an Egyptian inscription Ramesses II is said to have been a "chief of the army" when he was "a boy in the tenth year."[15] While the statement may contain an exaggeration, in that the title may have been merely honorific, there is no reason to doubt its essential validity, namely that the young prince had accompanied his father on the latter's military campaigns and been delegated some, perhaps minor, responsibility. By way of analogy we may note that Gideon's son, his first-born, Yether, accompanied his father on the military expedition which resulted in the capture of Zebah and Zalmunnah and that Gideon offered the boy what was no doubt the privilege of executing these enemy chiefs. The youngster did not draw his sword, the text relates, "because he was afraid, because he was yet a youngster."[16] And there is evidence, too, to suggest that Taharqa (biblical Tirhaqa, II Kings 19:9), when he led his Nubian forces in the abortive attempt to stay the Assyrian army under Sennacherib in 701 B.C.E., was probably in his teens.[17]

---

riage for Yasmaḫ-Addu (*ARM* I 24, 46, 77), since it may indicate that the boy was still under parental authority in such matters and too young to act for himself.

There is, in addition, an enigmatic statement by which Shamshi-Addu chides his son and which may point still further to the latter's extreme youth (*ARM* I 73:43 f., 108:6 f., 113:7 f.): *și-iḫ-re-et ú-ul eṭ-le-et ú-ul šar-tum i-na li-ti-ka*. The editor of the texts, G. Dossin, understands it to mean: "Thou art little, thou art not a man, thou hast no hair upon thy cheek!" For other interpretations of the statement see W. von Soden in *WO* I 193 and *CAD* IV (1958) 407 *b*.

[14] *ARM* I 69.

[15] J. H. Breasted, *Ancient Records of Egypt* (Chicago, 1906) III, § 288 (line 17).

[16] Judg. 8:20. It may also be of interest here to recall the words of (General) Othello, the Moor, in Shakespeare's play of that name (Act I, scene iii, lines 81–85, 128–33; italics mine):

> . . . Rude am I in my speech
> And little bless'd with the soft phrase of peace;
> For since these arms of mine had *seven* years' pith
> Till now some nine moons wasted, they have us'd
> Their dearest action in the tented field.
>
> Her father lov'd me, oft invited me;
> Still question'd me the story of my life
> From year to year—the battles, sieges, fortunes
> That I have pass'd.
> I ran it through, even *from my boyish days*
> To th' very moment that he bade me tell it.

[17] From Egyptian sources it is known that the Pharaoh of Egypt at this time was Shabaka, Taharqa's uncle, a fact which has led some to regard the biblical text as being in error (e.g. M. Noth, *The History of Israel* [trans. by S. Godman; London, 1958] p. 268). But Sennacherib, in that section of the annals concerned with his military activities in Palestine in 701,

Another line of argument appears from the observation that marriages in the ancient world (as in many nonurban societies of the modern world) generally took place between people of very young age, people in the middle to

states that Hezekiah had appealed for help to the kings of Egypt and Ethiopia and that he (Sennacherib) defeated them in the plain of Altaqu (*ANET*, pp. 267 f.). The Assyrian has here distinguished between Egypt and Ethiopia, and it is of interest to note that the Hebrew historian has referred to Taharqa not as king of Egypt nor yet as Pharaoh but as "king of Ethiopia," *melek Kush*.

Sometime after 701 Shabaka was succeeded on the throne of Egypt by his nephew Shebitku, who, in turn, was succeeded by his younger brother, Taharqa, in 689. Taharqa ruled for twenty-six years (see most recently, R. Parker, *Kush* VIII [1960] 268–69). In an inscription dated to his sixth year Taharqa relates that as "a goodly youth, a king's brother," he, in the company of other "goodly youths," came north (from Nubia) to Thebes to rejoin his brother Shebitku, who was then the reigning Pharaoh (M. F. Laming Macadam, *The Temples of Kawa* I [London, 1949] Inscr. IV 7 f.). In another inscription of "year 6" he tells that he had left his mother in Nubia when he was "a youth of twenty years when [he] came with His Majesty to lower Egypt." He goes on to say that "after an interval of years" his mother came to see him and found him crowned king of Egypt (*ibid.* Inscr. V 17–18). Macadam is of the opinion that Taharqa came north to join his brother on the throne of Egypt as coregent, that he numbered his regnal years from the start of his coregency, that Shebitku died about five years later, and that "year 6" was, in reality, Taharqa's first year as sole ruler (*ibid.* pp. 18–20, n. 30). If it be assumed with Macadam that Taharqa became coregent as a youth of twenty, and as it is known that he ruled for twenty-six years, then he would have been forty-six years of age at the time of his death in 664/663 and eight or nine years of age in 701. This calculation has led Macadam (*ibid.*) to reject the account in II Kings 19:9 as a manifest "mistake."

J. Leclant and J. Yoyotte, however, have argued cogently against Macadam's conjecture of a coregency of the two brothers. They point out that (1) Inscr. V 15 states explicitly that the successor of Shebitku had ascended the throne, had been crowned king, and had received his Horus name only after his predecessor's decease, (2) that Taharqa engaged in royal activities in Nubia and in Egypt from his second year, (3) that royal attributes are accorded him in texts and representations before his "year 6," and (4) that there exist private documents from Thebes dated according to his first years (*Bulletin de l'Institut français d'archéologie orientale* LI [1952] 24).

The coregency of Taharqa with his elder brother, Shebitku, being now generally regarded as unlikely (cf. *Les peuples de l'orient méditerranéen. II. L'Égypte*, par Étienne Drioton et Jacques Vandier [3 éd.; Paris, 1952] p. 548, n. 1), some interval of time must have elapsed between Taharqa's arrival at Thebes, when he was twenty years of age, and his first year of reign. To compute his age at death in 664/663, then, we must total 20 years (=his age on leaving his mother to join his brother), x years (=the interval between his arrival in Thebes and his enthronement in Memphis), and 26 years (=the length of his reign). In that inscription in which Taharqa tells that he was twenty years old when he came north at the bidding of the king, his brother (Inscr. V), he tells also that he "appeared" (i.e., became king) after his brother's death, that his mother came to see him "after an interval of years," and that she found him enthroned as king. It seems reasonable to assume that the visit of the queen mother had been occasioned not alone by the enthronement of her younger son but also by the death of the elder. If this assumption be valid, then the reference to the "interval of years" would correspond to the lapse of time between Taharqa's arrival in Thebes and his enthronement in Memphis, the "x" of our computation. The indefinite "interval of years" signifies a minimum of three years. If this minimum number, three

late teens. And since the heroes of legend, or warriors of the "heroic age," were frequently unmarried, or married but a short time, the implication inevitably follows that the heroes were in their early teens or younger. Evidence for teen-age marriage is not abundant, but it does exist. *Pirqe Aboth* (v 24), for example, sets the age for marriage at eighteen, while Rabbinic law forbids parents to give their children in marriage before the age of puberty yet urges them to do so as soon as this stage is reached.[18] And the Assyrian Laws (cf. § 43) permit marriage as early as the tenth year. Some evidence for teen-age marriage, moreover, is furnished by the Old Testament. In II Kings 21:19 it is told that Amon was twenty-two years old when he began to reign and that he reigned two years. At the end of that time, at age twenty-four, he was assassinated (verse 23). The rebellion having been quelled, his son Josiah was set on the throne. This son was eight years old when he began to rule (II Kings 22:1), a fact which indicates that Amon, his father, was sixteen years of age at the time of Josiah's birth and, therefore, that he married no later than his fifteenth year. In addition, Josiah, it is told, being eight years old when he began to reign and having reigned thirty-one years when he died, was thirty-nine years of age at the time of his death. His son, Jehoahaz, succeeded without incident to the throne at age twenty-three. If the biblical account is here correct, then Josiah was sixteen years old at the time of the birth of Jehoahaz and, as his father before him, therefore, had married no later than his fifteenth year.

Of the principal heroes of Homer's *Iliad*, Achilles is unmarried and Hector, though married, has only an infant child. Concerning Achilles there is, further-more, a legend extant which relates of the attempt on the part of Achilles' mother to prevent her son from participating in the war against Troy. This she does by having him disguised as a girl and harbored among the young women at the court of Lycomedes. To this court came the "wily" Odysseus on his assignment to locate the hero and, for this purpose, he carried with him a sword hidden among some woven goods. While the girls were engaged in inspecting the apparel, Achilles became engrossed in examining the sword. By this ruse, and this ruse alone, was Achilles' identity revealed and his disguise uncovered. The only age at which such successful deception is possible is before a boy

---

years, be taken to be the actual lapse of time, then Taharqa would have been forty-nine years old when he died in 664/663 and twelve or thirteen when he led his (Nubian = "Ethiopi-an") forces in 701. Since the indefinite "interval of years" can signify more than three years, however the chronology of Taharqa be resolved, it may be said that when he led his troops in the Battle of Altaqu in 701 he was certainly less than twenty years of age and more than twelve, i.e., he was in his teens. [I am greatly indebted to Dr. Edward F. Wente for refer-ences to Egyptological data and for several very valuable discussions pertaining to the problems surrounding the reign of Taharqa.]

[18] Sanh. 76 *b*.

acquires secondary male characteristics, that is to say, before the age of puberty.

In Mesopotamian literature, too, there are indications that military "heroes" were young and unmarried, that military activity preceded marriage. Witness the following excerpt from a Sumerian text referred to by Professor Thorkild Jacobsen as "The Lad in the Desert":

> Before the young wife was yet in his arms,
> And my mother might raise a (grand-)child on (her) knees;
> When (his) father- and mother-in-law had (just) thought of him
> And he had acquired them as father- and mother-in-law,
> When he was accepted among fellows as a friend,
>   when he was merely a young soldier,
> (Then) did (the powers) pass sentence upon him,
> On the noble young lord,
> And his god let the sentence befall him![19]

Extra-biblical examples can, but need not, be multiplied. It may suffice merely to cite two biblical figures who achieved fame for "heroic" physical and military prowess before their respective marriages, Samson and David. Samson's renowned physical exploits, it will be remembered, centered around his attempts at winning a bride, while it was not until David had gained fame as a successful military leader that marriage was proposed for him. In this connection it is highly significant that the Hebrew poet of the "Song of Deborah" should have envisaged the enemy commander's (Sisera's) mother as waiting anxiously for his return (Judg. 5:28–30) and not a wife.

Whatever, therefore, may have prompted the poet of Lamech's boast song to substitute for the traditional parallelism "man" // "son of Man" the unique parallelism "man" // "boy," there is no reason to doubt his intention or his meaning. Lamech is proud of his feat, the slaying of a boy, and we must no doubt understand by this a very young warrior, an upstart would-be hero.

---

[19] The translation is that of Thorkild Jacobsen in "Toward the Image of Tammuz," *History of Religions* I (1961) 201.

STUDY III

ISAAC'S BLESSING OVER JACOB[1]

THE long-standing rivalry between the neighboring peoples of Israel and Edom, beginning in the days of Moses, continued in the reigns of Saul, David, and Solomon, persisting throughout the biblical period, and climaxed in the year 70 c.e. with the Edomite (Idumean) participation in the fall of Jerusalem, finds reflection in the rivalry between their respective eponymous ancestors, the twin brothers Jacob-Israel and "Esau, he is Edom." Each of these twin brothers received a blessing from his father, the patriarch Isaac. The one intended for the elder, Esau, and mistakenly given to (or appropriated by) the younger, Jacob, was composed of three benedictions which, once pronounced, bestowed unalterably upon him agricultural fertility, political supremacy, and personal inviolability. The poet's association of these particular benefits within a single bequest was prompted, as we shall afterward contend, by a venerable tradition; this conglomeration of gifts was not a haphazard or ill-considered assemblage. On the other hand, as we shall furthermore argue, despite Isaac's statement in Gen. 27:37 and the judgment of several modern exegetes to the contrary, these favors did not constitute all that Isaac (or his tradition) had to bestow. Two items in particular are omitted. Since they are included elsewhere in the narrative, it may be said that, while the gifts were selected in accordance with tradition, they were distributed in accordance with design. That the Israelite poet of these blessings should have allowed his prejudice to influence his composition is readily appreciated; that he should have found means to utilize his tradition in the patterning of his poem to the end that Jacob very clearly is made the recipient of Isaac's blessing and Esau only apparently so is only to his credit. An analysis of the poem's structure will illustrate this.

I

The first of the blessings, bequeathing agricultural fertility, reads:

ויתן לך האלהים

מטל השמים ומשמני הארץ

ורב דגן ותירש

---

[1] Gen. 27:28–29.

And may God give thee
Of the dew of heaven, and of the fatness of the earth
And abundance of grain and wine.

While the elements "heaven" // "earth" and "dew" // "fatness" are separately known to recur in parallel elsewhere in biblical Hebrew poetry,[2] far more striking is the appearance of the parallelism of these "construct chains" in Ugaritic verse,[3] for it points to the antiquity of the poetic tradition which held the association of these terms in such relationship as fixed (*UM* ʿnt II 38–39 [=IV 87]):

תחספנ מה ותרחצ

טל שממ שמנ אר צ

She draws some water and washes
(With) the *dew of heaven*, the *fatness of earth*.

When, later, Isaac proceeded to "bless" Esau (Gen. 27:39), the phrases employed, though worded similarly, were altered in their order and in their meaning:

הנה מ‐שמני הארץ יהיה מושבך

ומ‐טל השמים מעל

Behold, (away) from the *fatness of earth* be thy dwelling,
And (away) from the *dew of heaven* above.

Such reversal in the succession of terms comprising a traditional parallel pair is of interest because, on the basis of existing evidence, the habit of the Syro-Palestinian poets in making use of fixed word-pairs in the construction of their verses appears to have been extended to the employment of these parallel terms in a specific or fixed order. When, therefore, inversions of traditional sequences occur, it becomes necessary to inquire concerning the significance of the alterations.

On occasion such aberrations may be accounted for by the application of a principle of compensation. That is to say, when a poet is found to have reversed the normal or regular succession of a traditionally fixed pair of parallel terms, he will often be found also to have appended an additional element to that term customarily located in the first of the parallel clauses which he has set in the second. To illustrate: twenty-five times in biblical Hebrew there occurs the parallelism עולם // דור דור , "forever" // "generation (upon) generation," in

---

[2] The parallel pair "heaven" // "earth" being so common in Old Testament literature, we need draw attention to only a few occurrences (Isa. 1:2 and 13:13, Hos. 2:23, Amos 9:6a) and see the studied use of this pair in Gen. 1:1 and 2:4.

On "dew" // "oil," see Ps. 133:2–3.

[3] Cf. H. L. Ginsberg, *The Ugarit Texts* (Jerusalem, 1936) p. 63 (Hebrew); *idem, ANET*, p. 136, n. 5.

this sequence. The antiquity of the tradition, to which such frequent use of the pair by a variety of authors attests, is confirmed by the appearance of this same pair five times in Ugaritic verse,[4] for example *UM* 1 Aqht 154:

ענת ברח פ- ע ל מ -ה

ענת פ- ד ר ד ר

Now . . . and *forever,*
Now and (for) *generation* (upon) *generation,*

and, as an example of its use by biblical authors, Exod. 3:15*b:*

זה שמי ל- ע ל ם

וזה זכרי ל- ד ר ד ר

This is my name *forever,*
And this my appellation for *generation* (upon) *generation.*

When the author of Ps. 45, employing this pair, chose to invert the traditional order of the parallelism, as he did in verse 18, he wrote:

אזכירה שמך בכל ד ר ו- ד ר

על כן עמים יהודך ל- ע ל ם ועד

I shall cause thy name to be remembered in every *generation* (upon) *generation,*
So that peoples shall praise thee *forever* and ever.

To the term עלם, "forever," which, as we have noted, is so regularly found as the first of the parallel pair, the poet, having here set it in second position, has appended the additional term ועד, "and ever."

Again, the fixed pair (צר(ר) // אויב, "enemy" // "foe," which occurs with some frequency in this sequence, for example, in Ugaritic, *UM* ᶜnt IV 48:[5]

מנם א ב יפע לבעל

צ ר ת לרכב ערפת

What *enemy* hath risen against Baal?
(What) *foe* against the Rider of the Clouds?

and in Hebrew, for example, Ps. 81:15:[6]

כמעט א ו י ב י -הם אכניע

ועל צ ר י -הם אשיב ידי

Shortly would I humble their *enemies,*
And against their *foes* would turn my hand,

---

[4] Cf. *JNES* XX 43, Table 1, No. 2; Cassuto, *The Goddess Anath,* p. 24; Ginsberg, *Journal of the Palestine Oriental Society* XV (1935) 327.

[5] *JNES* XX 44, Table 1, No. 3; Cassuto, *Tarbiz* XIV 3.

[6] *JNES* XX 44, Table 1, No. 3.

appears in reverse sequence in Ps. 89:43:[7]

הרימות ימין צריו

השמחת כל אויביו

Thou hast exalted the right hand of his *foes*,
Thou hast gladdened all his *enemies*,

where again it may be noted that to the term found ordinarily in first position and now placed in second position has been added another element, here in construct relation, "all."

More often, and of greater significance in the present context, it is found that the poet will have reversed the customary succession of terms when he has already employed the fixed pair in the traditional sequence, that is to say, when the pairs follow hard upon one another either in fact or in meaning. The poet thus creates, as it were, a chiasmus. In illustration of this we may note the parallelism ארץ // עפר, "earth "// "dust," which is regular in Old Testament as in Ugaritic verse, appearing in this order thirteen times in biblical Hebrew and ten times in Ugaritic,[8] for example *UM* 76 II 24–25:

נטען ב- א ר צ אבי

וב- ע פ ר קם אֿחכ

We shall nail my enemies in the *earth*,
And in the *dust* those who rise against thy brother,

and Isa. 34:7*b:*

ורותה א ר צ -ם מדם

ו- ע פ ר -ם מחלב ידשן

And their *earth* shall be drenched with blood,
And their *dust* shall be glutted with fat.

When the biblical writer of the latter passage wished to repeat the parallelism (verse 9), he wrote:

ונהפכו נחליה לזפת ו- ע פ ר -ה ל נפרית

והיתה א ר צ -ה לזפת בערה

And her wadis shall be turned to pitch, and her *dust* to sulphur,
And her *earth* shall become burning pitch.

---

[7] Cf. particularly Mic. 5:8.

[8] *JNES* XX 43, Table 1, No. 1; Cassuto, *The Goddess Anath*, p. 24; Ginsberg, *Bulletin of the Jewish Palestine Exploration Society* III (1935) 55.

Or, again, the parallelism יין // שכר, "wine" // "beer," known thus far only in biblical Hebrew poetry,[9] occurs regularly in this sequence.[10] Twice, when the order of terms is inverted, the inversion follows immediately upon the regular succession of these words in parallelism, Isa. 28:7:

וגם אלה ב-יין שגו

וב-ש כ ר תעו

כהן ונביא שגו ב-ש כ ר

נבלעו מן ה-יין

And even these reel from *wine*,
And stagger from *beer:*

Priest and prophet reel from *beer*,
Are confused by *wine*,

and Prov. 31:4, 6:

אל למלכים שתו יין

ולרוזנים או ש כ ר

תנו ש כ ר לאובד

ו-יין למרי נפש

It is not for kings to drink *wine*,
Or for rulers (to drink) *beer;*

Give *beer* to the one who perisheth,
And *wine* to the embittered of soul.[11]

The Ugaritic poet, too, on occasion could make effective use of this tradition. Thus, when the artisan god *Kṯr-w-Ḫss* suggests to Baal that a "win-

[9] Unless it is to be recognized in *UM* 2 Aqht I 31–32 (cf. *UM* 2 Aqht II 19–20):

א[חֹ]ד ידה ב-ש כ ר ן

מעמסה [כ]שבע י ן

Who taketh his hand when he is *drunken*,
Who carrieth him [when] he is sated with *wine*,

in reverse sequence with compensation.

[10] Isa. 5:22, 24:9, 28:7, 29:9, 56:12; Prov. 20:1. Cf. also Num. 6:3, Deut. 14:26, Mic. 2:11. The text of Isa. 5:11 is difficult; cf. Isa. 5:12. For this pair in reverse sequence with compensation, see Joel 1:5.

[11] Chiasmus, though frequent, is not always employed when the pair succeeds itself; cf. the parallelism "earth" // "dust" in Isa. 29:4.

dow" // "casement" be constructed in his (Baal's) house (*UM* 51 V 123–24[12]):

בל אשת א ר ב ת בבה[תמ]

ח ל נ בקרב הכלמ

A *window* let me set in the hou[se],
A *casement* in the midst of the palace,

Baal at first refuses, using the same pair in the same sequence, *UM* 51 V 126–27:[13]

אל תשת א ר ב ת ב[בהתמ]

[ח ל]נ בקרב הכ[למ]

Set not a *window* in [the house],
[A *caseme*]nt in the midst of the pala[ce].

Later, when Baal changes his mind, the words of the parallel pair are inverted, *UM* 51 VII 17–19:[14]

יפתח ח ל נ בבהתמ

א ר [ב] ת בקרב הכלמ

Let a *casement* be opened in the house,
A *win[dow]* in the midst of the palace.

When, therefore, Isaac came to bless Esau, employing the same fixed parallelism that he had employed in his benediction over Jacob, "dew of heaven" // "fatness of earth," it may well have been tradition that had prescribed the inversion of phrases. Nevertheless, it does not appear possible to ignore the implication that the author of this passage, by his skillful use of tradition in reversing the parallelism, may have intended thereby to reverse the blessing as well.

II

The second of the three blessings which Isaac unwittingly pronounced upon Jacob, bequeathing political supremacy, is itself separable into two parts. The first reads:

יעבדוך עמים

וישתחו לך לאמים

May peoples serve thee,
And populations bow down to thee.

Each of the two sets of parallel terms recurs in biblical Hebrew with sufficient frequency to be regarded as fixed and traditional pairs. For instance the pair

[12] Cf. *UM* 51 VI 5–6.
[13] Cf. *UM* 51 VI 8–9.
[14] Cf. *UM* 51 VII 25–27.

עַם // לְאֹם, "people" // "population," is found again in Ps. 57:10:

אודך ב-ע מ י ם אדני
אזמרך ב-ל א מ י ם

I shall praise thee among the *peoples*, O my lord,
I shall sing of thee among the *populations*,

in Prov. 14:28:

ברב ע ם הדרת מלך
ובאפס ל א ם מחתת ׳רוזן׳[15]

In a multitude of *people* is the glory of a king,
And in the lack of *population* is the ruin of a ⸢ruler⸣,[15]

and several more times.[16]

The verbs עבד // השתחוה, "serve" // "bow down," in this order, though encountered rarely in poetry, in prose are often associated,[17] for example I Kings 22:54*a*:

ו-יע ב ד את הבעל
ו-ישתחוה לו

And he *served* the Baal,
And he *bowed down* to him,

Deut. 29:25*a*:

וילכו ו-יע ב ד ו אלהים אחרים
ו-ישתחוו להם

And they went and they *served* other gods,
And they *bowed down* to them.

In a clearly poetic passage (Ps. 72:11) the pair occurs in reverse sequence:[18]

ו-ישתחוו לו כל מלכים
כל גוים יע ב ד ו-הו

And may all kings *bow down* to him,
All nations *serve* him.

Before the decipherment of Ugaritic the verb השתחוה was considered to have been derived from a root שחה. In order to explain the appearance of two

[15] Cf. *BH, ad loc.*, n., and p. 3, n. 11, above, for references to the parallelism ⸢king⸣ // ⸢ruler.⸣

[16] Isa. 17:12, 51:4; Jer. 51:58; Hab. 2:13; Ps. 47:4, 57:10, 67:5, 108:4; Prov. 14:28, 24:24. Cf. also Isa. 55:4, reading with the versions.

[17] Deut. 8:19, 11:16, 29:25; Josh. 23:16; Judg. 2:19; I Kings 9:6, 22:54; Jer. 13:10, 16:11, 25:6; II Chron. 7:19.

[18] Cf. Exod. 20:5, 23:24; Deut. 4:19, 5:9, 30:17; I Kings 9:9; II Kings 17:16; Jer. 22:9; II Chron. 7:22, 33:3.

final weak consonants, שחוה, the stem was judged to be *hiṯpaʿlēl*.[19] The verb occurs in Ugaritic in the forms ישתחוי, ישתחוין, and תשתחוי,[20] spellings which indicate that the final *yodh* is an element of the root and that the verb in both languages, therefore, is to be analyzed as the *Št* stem of the root חוי.[21] This being so, we may then remark in Isaac's words to Esau, Gen 27:40:

ועל חרבך תחיה

ואת אחיך תעבד

By (upon?) thy sword shalt thou *live* (bow?),
And thy brother shalt thou *serve*,

by a highly probable play on the verbal roots חוי and חיי, a reversal of the sequence of the parallel pair עבד // (השת)חוי. Were this to prove correct, we would have another instance in these blessings of an inversion of parallelism to help fashion a reversal of meaning.

Reinforcing the bequest of sovereignty just bestowed upon Jacob, the poet adds the following benediction:

הוה גביר לאחיך

וישתחוו לך בני אמך

Be lord over thy brothers,
And may thy mother's sons bow down to thee.

The plural forms "brothers" // "mother's sons" have created for modern interpreters of the passage considerable misgiving, for, as is repeatedly stressed by these scholars, Isaac and Rebecca are nowhere said to have borne other children. The use of these plurals would thus appear, at first blush, to be a serious oversight on the part of the poet. Some have therefore opined that the situation as described in the prose narrative has here been forgotten,[22] while others have suggested that the poem had existed independently of the narrative into which it was later inserted.[23] But such niceties fail to take into account other references in the text of Genesis to Jacob's brothers, as Gen. 27:37:

And Isaac answered and said to Esau, "Behold, I have made him [Jacob] thy lord, and *all his brothers* have I given to him for servants,"

and Gen. 31:46:

And Jacob said to *his brothers*, "Gather stones."

[19] GKC, § 75 *kk.*

[20] For a complete listing see G. Douglas Young, *Concordance of Ugaritic* ("Analecta Orientalia" XXXVI [Roma, 1956]) p. 27.

[21] Cf. Ginsberg, *The Ugarit Texts*, p. 145; C. H. Gordon, *UM*, § 20:619.

[22] Skinner, *A Critical and Exegetical Commentary on Genesis*, p. 372.

[23] C. A. Simpson, "The Book of Genesis," *The Interpreter's Bible* I (New York, 1952) 683 f., commentary on verse 29.

However the problem of the plurality of Jacob's brothers be resolved, from the standpoint of the poetic craft the association of the terms "brother(s)" and "mother's son(s)" in parallel clauses was a traditional feature of Syro-Palestinian verse. In Old Testament literature one remarks its appearance in Ps. 50:20:

תשב ב-א ח י ך תדבר

ב-ב ן א מ ך תתן דפי

Thou dost sit (? and) against thy *brother* dost speak,
Against thy *mother's son* dost give out slander,

Ps. 69:9:

⟨כ⟩מו²⁴ זר הייתי ל-א ח י

ונכרי ל-ב נ י א מ י

Like a stranger[24] have I become to my *brothers*,
And a foreigner to my *mother's sons*.

In apposition the traditionally parallel terms may be noted in Deut. 13:7:

כי יסיתך אחיך בן אמך

If thy *brother*, thy *mother's son*, . . . entice thee,

Judg. 8:19*a:*

ויאמר אחי בני אמי הם

And he said, "My *brothers*, my *mother's sons*, (were) they."

In Ugaritic verse the pair occurs three times:[25]

UM 49 VI 10–11 (= 14–15):

אַחִים יתנ בעל לפאָי

ב נ מ אָ מ י כלי י

My *brothers* hath Baal given . . .
My *mother's sons* . . . ,

UM Krt 8–9:

דשבע]אַ[חֹ מ לה

תֹמנת ב נ אָ מ

Who had seven [bro]*thers,*
Eight *mother's sons.*

The parallelism of the verbs in these cola, "be (lord)" // "bow down," is not otherwise attested. Nevertheless, there is evident here a pattern of verbs in structured parallelism to which attention must be drawn. In the preceding

²⁴ Cf. p. 10 above.
²⁵ Cf. Ginsberg, *The Legend of King Keret*, p. 33, commentary on line 9.

couplet the verbs set in parallel relationship, "serve" // "bow down," it was
seen, constituted a traditional pair for the Hebrew poets. The second term of
that pair finds employment again in the present couplet, and again as the
second term. The pattern of verbs appearing in these two couplets, then, is
"serve" // "bow down" (//) "be (lord)" // "bow down," which may be represented schematically as *a* // *b* (//) *c* // *b*. This pattern is current elsewhere in
biblical Hebrew poetry and may be regarded as a regular feature of it. For example, the parallelism of the verbs "hear" // "give ear," shown above (p. 27)
to have been traditional, occurs, among other places, in Isa. 28:23, where it is
coupled with yet another verb, הקשיב, "attend":

האזינו ו-שמעו קולי

הקשיבו ו- שמעו אמרתי

Give ear and *hear* my voice,
Attend and *hear* my speech!

The same pattern is clearly discernible, namely "give ear" // "hear" // "attend" // "hear" or, schematically, *a* // *b* // *c* // *b*. Since this pattern of verbs
in parallel structure may be noted repeatedly in Old Testament poetic texts—
for example with another pair of traditionally parallel verbs, יצר // ברא,
"fashion" // "create," in Isa. 45:7:[26]

יוצר אור

ו-בורא חשך

עשה שלום

ו-בורא רע

The one who *fashioneth* light
And who *createth* darkness,
Who *maketh* well-being
And who *createth* evil,

where the parallelism "fashion" // "create" // "make" // "create" again
forms the scheme *a* // *b* // *c* // *b*—it may be recognized as yet another device
in the repertoire of Hebrew poetic diction and help mitigate considerably the
arguments of those who would divide these two couplets of the second blessing
between two distinct authors.

III

The anticipated effect of the last of the three benedictions pronounced by
Isaac upon Jacob is unconditional physical and spiritual protection. Malediction in the ancient world was a widely recognized means for harming another
and had, in addition, prohibitive and protective functions.[27] By cursing any

[26] Cf. e.g. Isa. 43:1, 45:18; Amos 4:13.

[27] For the prohibitive/protective function of malediction, cf. the writer's study "West-
Semitic Curses and the Problem of the Origins of Hebrew Law," *VT* XI (1961) 137 ff.

possible future imprecator of his son, Isaac sought to insure him against hurt:

ארריך ארור

ומברכיך ברוך

Cursed be those who curse thee,
And blessed be those who bless thee.

Two elements of literary tradition are in evidence here: the fixed pair "curse" //
"bless" and the duplication of the parallelism.

The traditional character of the pair "curse" // "bless" may be acknowl-
edged from its recurrence in Jer. 20:14:

א ר ו ר היום אשר ילדתי בו

יום אשר ילדתני אמי אל יהי ב ר ו ך

Cursed be the day on which I was born,
The day my mother bore me, let it not *be blessed*,

and Prov. 3:33:

מ א ר ת יהוה בבית רשע

ונוה צדיקים י ב ר ך

Yhwh's *curse* is on the house of the wicked,
But the dwelling of the righteous doth he *bless*.

Compare also Jer. 17:5, 7:

א ר ו ר הגבר אשר יבטח באדם

ב ר ו ך הגבר אשר יבטח ביהוה

Cursed be the man who trusteth in Man,
Blessed be the man who trusteth in Yhwh.

In prose the pair is found in Num. 22:12:[28]

לא ת א ר את העם

כי ב ר ו ך הוא

Thou shalt not *curse* this people,
For it is *blessed*.

With the order of terms reversed the parallelism may be noted in Num. 24:9:

מברכיך ב ר ו ך

ו-א ר ר י ך ארור

Blessed be those who *bless* thee,
And *cursed be* those who *curse* thee,

---

[28] Cf. also Gen. 12:3, Judg. 5:23–24, Mal. 2:2.

and in prose in Num. 22:6:

כי ידעתי את אשר תברך מברך

ואשר תאר יואר

For I know that whom thou dost *bless* is *blessed*,
And whom thou dost *curse* is *cursed*.

Duplication of a fixed pair in parallel cola finds expression elsewhere in Syro-Palestinian literature, for example in the inscription of Azitawada, king of Adana, where, in the introduction to the imprecation, we find the repeated parallelism מלך // רזן, "king" // "ruler," noted above (p. 3, n. 11) as a traditional parallel pair:

ואם מלכ ב-מלכם

ו-רזנ ב-רזנם

And if a *king* among *kings*,
Or *ruler* among *rulers*. . . .

Having shown that the blessing Isaac pronounced upon his son Jacob was constructed entirely in accordance with the traditions of Syro-Palestinian poetic composition and that these traditions were ably manipulated by the Israelite poet in such a way as to enhance Jacob and to eclipse Esau, we have yet to discuss and to attempt to elucidate the significance of this threefold benediction.

When Esau returned from fulfilling his father's wish, having hunted and prepared the desired food, he requested the blessing promised him. On being told that the benediction had already been given his brother, Esau asked whether his father had not reserved a blessing for him and was told:

Behold, I have made him [Jacob] lord over thee, and all his brothers have I given to him for servants, and (with) grain and wine have I sustained him. And where is that which I may do for thee, my son?

Many have read into this rhetorical question the implication that there was in reality nothing else wherewith to bless the disappointed son, Esau. Yet, at the beginning of the following chapter (Gen. 28:3), Isaac, sending Jacob to the home of the latter's maternal grandfather, pronounced upon him still another benediction:

And may God Allmighty bless thee and make thee fruitful, and multiply thee; and mayest thou become an assembly of peoples.

By this, Isaac had in addition blessed Jacob with human fertility. Even so, he had not yet exhausted all the categories of tradition's entire stock of benisons. While this assertion is not readily demonstrable from an investigation of ancient benedictions extant (the number of them is too few and their contents too restricted), examination of this genre's counterpart, malediction, does afford such an opportunity, for examples of this are numerous and their contents less restrained. Furthermore, those things considered important enough wherewith one might be blessed are the very things tradition found important enough wherewith one might be cursed. By subjection of the latter to content analysis, therefore, there is provided—in so far as the religio-literary genres benediction and malediction are, as appears self-evident, antithetic—the necessary key for the understanding of the significance attaching to the particular compilation and distribution of the patriarch's blessings.

Analysis of the motifs expressed in imprecations extant from the ancient world reveals that they fall readily into three major (or six minor) categories: human and agricultural fertility, governmental and military sovereignty, physical and spiritual salubrity.[29] If, as seems most probable, these are also the very things with which tradition prescribed one might be blessed, then Isaac's benediction over Jacob may be seen to have been quite artfully composed (by the author of the passage) of a cluster of benisons very carefully selected. For Jacob was here the recipient of agricultural fertility, governmental sovereignty, and personal—that is, physical and spiritual—inviolability, favors which clearly were originally intended for Esau and which, under his mother's promptings, Jacob usurped. The bequest of human fertility later bestowed upon Jacob, then, the author doubtless implies, was specifically intended for him. Yet the same pro-Israelite storyteller seems deliberately to have refrained from granting Jacob the one remaining category of benediction from tradition's store (and by this, perhaps, interprets Israel's history as he knew it), namely, military sovereignty. This he reserved for, and willed to, Esau, but in so questionable a manner—"by (upon?) thy sword shalt thou live (bow?)"—as hardly, from the biblical point of view, to be construed as a blessing at all.

---

[29] For this analysis see the writer's "Curse Motifs in the Old Testament and in the Ancient Near East" (unpublished Ph.D. dissertation, Department of Oriental Languages and Civilizations, University of Chicago, 1959) particularly pp. 120–99.

STUDY IV

BALAAM'S FIRST "MASHAL"[1]

WHEN the Children of Israel had completed their wanderings in the wilderness and had effected certain military victories over Amorites living in the region between the Arnon and Jabbok rivers in Trans-Jordan, they proceeded to encamp in Moabite territory opposite Jericho. The king of Moab, Balak, son of Zippor, fearful of the Israelites' designs and uncertain of his ability to repel them successfully, solicited the aid of the sorcerer Balaam, son of Beor. Promising substantial reward for his services, Balak bade Balaam curse the people of Israel to the end that they might thereby be rendered ineffectual and thus vulnerable to attack. Balaam, however, prompted by YHWH, instead pronounced a series of *meshalim* which served rather to frustrate Balak's intent.

The first *mashal*, with which we shall be primarily concerned, is composed of seven pairs of parallel cola. Except for the seventh, which I find incomprehensible, these form a coherent whole which may be summed up in prosaic fashion as Balaam's statement of the invulnerability of Israel to sorcery. In the several couplets he tells (1) that he was brought by Balak (2) to curse Israel; (3) that he cannot curse if God has not cursed; (4) that when he looks at the people, Israel, he finds that (5) it is safe and secure and (6) that therefore no one is able to bewitch Israel.

I

The first couplet (Num. 23:7*ba*) reads:

מן ארם ינחני בלק
מלך מואב מהררי קדם

From Aram did Balak fetch me,
The king of Moab from the Mountains of Qedem.

Though readily separable, the elements in parallel, "Aram" // "Mountains of Qedem" and "Balak" // "king of Moab," do not constitute what have been termed "fixed pairs"; that is to say, they are not again in extant sources found in parallel relationship. The general pattern governing the construction of each of these pairs, however, is sufficiently well attested to permit us to recognize a poetic tradition functioning here as well. Thus, noting that the first pair is

[1] Num. 23:7–10.

composed of a territorial appellation, "Aram," paralleled by a geographic designation, "Mountains of Qedem," we may compare it with other similar constructions, for example that in another early poem, Joshua's invocation to the sun
and moon, Josh. 10:12:

שמש ב-גבעון דום

וירח ב-עמק אילון

Sun, in *Gibeon* be still,
And moon, in the *Valley of Ajalon,*[2]

that in Amos 1:5:

ושברתי בריח דמשק

והכרתי יושב מ-בקעת און

And I shall break the bar of *Damascus,*
And shall cut off the inhabitant from the *Vale of Awen,*

and that in Ps. 78:43:

אשר שם ב-מצרים אתותיו

ומופתיו ב-שדה צען

When he put his signs in *Egypt,*
And his portents in the *Fields of Zoan.*

The pattern is furthermore attested in Ugaritic verse, for example *UM* 67 V
18–19:[3]

יְאָהב עגלת ב-דבר

פרת ב-שד שחלממת

He loveth a calf in *Dbr,*
A heifer in the *Field of Šḥlmmt.*

In the same way may the parallelism of the name of the ruler, "Balak," with his
title, "king of Moab," be compared, for example, with that in Isa. 41:21:

קרבו ריבכם יאמר יהוה

הגישו עצמותיכם יאמר מלך יעקב

"Set forth your case," saith *YHWH,*
"Bring forth your proofs," saith the *king of Jacob.*

To a similar pattern of parallelism we have already (p. 26) applied the term
"epithetic" parallelism, which may perhaps serve here as well.

[2] The parallelism "sun" // "moon" in this poem was traditional. Note its occurrence in
Isa. 13:10*b*, 60:19*a* and 20*a;* Jer. 31:35*a;* Ezek. 32:7*b;* Joel 3:4*a;* Ps. 72:5, 121:6, 136:8*a*
and 9*a.* Cf. also perhaps Deut. 33:14, Hab. 3:10–11 (reading with Septuagint), Ps. 89:37*b*–
38*a.* In reverse order the pair occurs in Ps. 104:19.

[3] Cf. *UM* 67 VI 6–7, 29–30; *UM* 49 II 19–20.

A comparable phenomenon is to be noted in the opening lines of each of the remaining three *meshalim;* that is to say, the specific elements ordered here in parallel cola, though for the most part not again found in such relationship, are nevertheless demonstrably traditional in structure. Thus, the second *mashal* (Num. 23:18b) opens:

קום בלק ושמע

האזינה עדי בנו צפר

Arise Balak and hear,
Give ear to my testimony(?) O Son of Zippor.

While the verbs "hear" // "give ear" constitute a fixed pair, as has been shown above (p. 27), the parallelism "Balak" // "son of Zippor" occurs only here. The pattern of the construction that may be abstracted, however, "PN₁" // "son of PN₂,"[4] is found again in another early poem, Sheba's call to revolution, II Sam. 20:1:[5]

אין לנו חלק ב-ד ו ד

ולא נחלה לנו ב-ב ן י ש י

We have no portion in *David*,
Nor have we any inheritance in the *son of Jesse*,

as also in Amos 1:4:

ושלחתי אש בבית ח ז א ל

ואכלה ארמנות ב ן ה ד ד

And I shall send a fire against the house of *Hazael*,
And it shall consume the palaces of the *son of Hadad*.

The same pattern may be noted, furthermore, in still another early poem (Judg. 5:12b), where we find "Barak" // "son of Abinoam." That this parallelistic construction was traditional in Syro-Palestinian literature may be deduced from its appearance, moreover, in Ugaritic poetry. The name of the hero "Aqhat," for instance, has as its parallel the patronymic "son of Danil,"

---

[4] E. Z. Melamed regards this as a breakup of a stereotyped prosaic phrase; cf. *Tarbiz* XVI (1945) 186 f.

[5] Cf. I Sam. 25:10 and I Chron. 12:19. The remaining pair of this early poem, "portion" // "inheritance," is also traditional. Cf. Job 20:29, 27:13, 31:2; perhaps also Deut. 32:9; Jer. 10:16, 51:19; less certainly Num. 18:20; Joel 4:2b; Ps. 16:5-6; Josh. 19:51. Note too its occurrence in the newly discovered Qumran "War Scroll," col. xii 11.

UM 3 Aqht 18–19:[6]

אַקהת כמ יתֹב ללחמ

ו- בנ דנאֶל לתֹרמ

Aqhat as he sitteth to eat,
The *son of Danil* to dine,

as the name of the deity "Baal" is paralleled by "son of Dagan,"

UM 49 I 22–24:

ל ירֹט עמ ב ע ל

ל יעדב מרח עמ בנ דגנ

He cannot run with *Baal*,
He cannot cast(?) spear with the *son of Dagan*,

UM 76 III 14–15:[7]

ב ע ל יתֹב לכס]אֶ[

בנ דגנ לכח]תֹ[

Baal sitteth upon (his) thro[ne],
The *son of Dagan* upon (his) chai[r].

Just so does tradition appear to have influenced the formulation of the introductory lines of the third and fourth *meshalim*, Num. 24:3b and 15b:

נאם בלעם בנו בער

ונאם הגבר שתם העין

The oracle of Balaam, son of Beor,
And the oracle of the man whose eye is perfect(?),[8]

since it is difficult to dissociate them from the structurally identical statement introducing the "last words of David," II Sam. 23:1b:

נאם דוד בן ישי

ונאם הגבר הקם על

The oracle of David, son of Jesse,
And the oracle of the man raised on high(?).[9]

---

[6] Cf. *UM* 3 Aqht 29–30.

[7] Similarly, *UM* 62:6–7 (=67 VI 23–24); 75 I 38–39; 76 III 12–13, 14–15; 137:35 (=137:18–19), 36–37; Krt 77–79 (=Krt 169–71).

[8] On this very difficult phrase see Albright, *JBL* LXIII (1944) 216 f., nn. 56–57. With reservations cf. J. M. Allegro, *VT* III (1953) 78 f.

[9] On the difficulty of this phrase see H. P. Smith, *A Critical and Exegetical Commentary on the Books of Samuel* ("International Critical Commentary" [Edinburgh, 1899]) p. 382. S.

When examined in the light of one another the formulaic character of these introductory statements is immediately apparent and may be schematized:

The oracle (נאם) of PN$_1$, son of PN$_2$,

And the oracle (ונאם) of the man (הגבר) + a distinguishing characteristic(?).

However the final clauses be understood and whatever the relationship between these two introductions, the conclusion that they are instances of the same literary tradition seems unavoidable.

II–III

In the second couplet the sorcerer-poet, purporting to quote the words of Balak, states the reason for his having been brought, that is to say, the assignment given him by the Moabite ruler, Num. 23:7$b\beta$:

לכה ארה לי יעקב
ולכה זעמה ישראל

Go! Curse for me Jacob!
And go! Denounce Israel!

The parallel designation of the people, "Jacob" // "Israel," has been the subject of considerable misapprehension. A. F. von Gall argued that the term "Jacob" as it is used in these poems of Balaam, where it is always in parallel with "Israel," must refer to the whole people and that such usage is confined to late biblical sources. In early biblical books (e.g. Amos), he continued, the term "Jacob," when it refers to the people and not to the patriarch, signifies the northern kingdom alone.[10] The argument may be effectively refuted by reference to and analysis of Mic. 3:1, 8, 9 and Isa. 2:6 and need detain us no longer.[11] Far more curious, however, are such statements by other writers as the following:

This usage [the parallelism "Jacob" // "Israel"] is frequent in all the Balaam oracles. It is found elsewhere in the Pent. *only* in Ex. xix. 3; and in the Blessing of Moses (Dt. xxxiii. 4, 10, 28). Other writers who use it are Micah (four times) and Isaiah xl.–lv. (seventeen times).[12]

Mowinckel in *ZAW* XLV (1927) 32, instead of the Massoretic text's *huqam ʿāl*, reads *hēqîm ʿelyôn*. Taking it to be a relative clause, he renders "whom Elyon has established": "(Worte) des Mannes den Eljon aufgestellt, d.h. in sein Amt eingesetzt hat."

[10] A. F. von Gall, "Zusammensetzung und Herkunft der Bileam-Perikope in Num. 22–24," *Festgruss Bernhard Stade* (Giessen, 1900) pp. 19–22.

[11] Cf. J. Mauchline, "The Balaam-Balak Songs and Saga," *Presentation Volume to William Barron Stevenson* ("Studia Semitica et Orientalia" II [Glasgow, 1945]) pp. 75 f.

[12] L. Elliott Binns, *The Book of Numbers* ("Westminster Commentaries" [ed. by W. Lock; London, 1927]) p. 161.

The parallelism of Jacob and Israel is noteworthy, for *it is used rarely* (see Exod. 19:3; Deut. 33:4–5, 10, 28; Micah; II Isaiah).[13]

These statements (the italics are mine) are patently false. The parallelism "Jacob" // "Israel" occurs three times in the Book of Genesis in the "Blessing of Jacob,"

Gen. 49:2:

הקבצו ושמעו בני י ע ק ב

ושמעו אל י ש ר א ל אביכם

Gather together and hear, O sons of *Jacob*,
And hearken to *Israel* your father,

Gen. 49:7*b:*

אחלקם ב-י ע ק ב

ואפיצם ב-י ש ר א ל

I shall sunder them in *Jacob*,
And shall scatter them in *Israel*,

Gen. 49:24*b:*

מידי אביר י ע ק ב

משם רעה אבן י ש ר א ל

. . . the mighty one of *Jacob*,
. . . the stone(?) of *Israel*,

and is one of the most frequently encountered parallel pairs in Old Testament literature, occurring more than fifty times in the sequence "Jacob" // "Israel"[14] and six times in reverse sequence.[15] Moreover, the fact that it was employed

[13] John Marsh, "The Book of Numbers," *The Interpreter's Bible* II (New York, 1953) 255, commentary on verse 7*b*. This remark would seem to have been based on a misunderstanding of an observation made by George Buchanan Gray, *A Critical and Exegetical Commentary on the Book of Numbers* ("International Critical Commentary" [New York, 1903]) p. 346: "The frequent use of the parallelism is characteristic of two other writers only, viz. Isaiah 40–55 (17 times) and Micah 1–3 (4 times)."

[14] Gen. 49:2, 7*b*, 24*b;* Exod. 19:3*bβ*; Num. 23:7, 10, 21, 23 and 24:5, 17; Deut. 33:10*a;* II Sam. 23:1*b;* Isa. 9:7, 14:1*aα*, 27:6*a*, 29:23*b*, 40:27*a*, 41:14*a*, 42:24, 43:1*a*, 22, and 28*b*, 44:1, 5, 21*a*, and 23*b*, 45:4*a*, 46:3*a*, 48:1*aα* and 12*a*, 49:5*aβ* and 6*aβ;* Jer. 2:4, 10:16, 30:10*aα* (=46:27); Ezek. 39:25*aβ*; Hos. 12:13; Mic. 1:5, 2:12*aα*, 3:1*a*, 8*b*, and 9*a;* Nah. 2:3*a;* Ps. 14:7*b* (=53:7*b*), 22:24, 78:5*a*, 21, and 71, 105:10 (=I Chron. 16:17); II Kings 17:34.

[15] Deut. 33:28; Isa. 41:8*a;* Ps. 81:5, 105:23, 114:1; I Chron. 16:13. Cf. also Isa. 10:20 and Ezek. 20:5.

by such early authors as Hosea, for example Hos. 12:13:

ויברח יעקב שדה ארם

ויעבד ישראל באשה

And *Jacob* fled to the fields of Aram,
And *Israel* served for a woman,

with obvious reference to the patriarch and by others with reference to the northern kingdom (e.g. Amos 3:13–14), to the southern kingdom (Mic. 3:1, 8, 9), and to the whole people (Gen. 49:7*b*) indicates that the parallelism of the terms was itself traditional and quite independent of any specific allusion the individual names might, by a particular poet, be made to bear. The imputation of any explicit referent underlying either or both of the words in parallel was manifestly at the discretion of the author. So much was this so that the poet might even, by creating two distinct contexts, attribute two quite different values to the same parallel pair within the very same poem. Witness the excerpts from the "Blessing of Jacob" (Gen. 49) cited above, where, in the first quotation reference is to the patriarch, while in the second it is to the people. Furthermore, for the eighth-century prophet Hosea, the parallelism "Jacob" // "Israel" was apparently so traditional that he could set in parallel relation the verbal "roots" from which these names were popularly derived,[16] Hos. 12:4:

בבטן עקב את אחיו

ובאונו שרה את אלהים

In the womb he *overreached* his brother,
And in his manhood *strove* with God.

The occurrence of this parallelism elsewhere in the Balaam poems is furthermore worthy of note since the pair is used clearly six times and is probably to be reconstructed in a seventh instance.[17] It is twice coupled with other fixed pairs, Num. 23:21*a*:

לא הביט און ב-יעקב

ולא ראה עמל ב-ישראל

Mischief is not noted in *Jacob*,
Nor is villainy seen in *Israel*,[18]

---

[16] See the popular etymologies accorded these names in Gen. 25:26 and 32:28 respectively.

[17] Cf. Albright, *JBL* LXIII 221 and n. 94.

[18] The parallelism *hibbiṭ* // *rāʾā* occurs ten times in this sequence: I Sam. 17:42; II Kings 3:14*b*; Isa. 5:12*b*, 22:8*b*–9*a* and 11*b*, 63:15*a*; Ps. 33:13, 91:8; Job 28:24; I Chron. 21:21. The pair occurs seven times in this sequence though not in parallelism: Isa. 42:18, Ps. 22:18, 80:15, and 142:5, Job 35:5, Lam. 1:12 and 5:1; five times in parallelism in reverse sequence:

and Num. 24:5:

מה טבו אהליך יעקב

משכנתיך ישראל

How lovely are thy tents, O *Jacob*,
Thy dwelling-places, O *Israel*.[19]

The remaining pair in Balaam's second couplet, ארר // זעם, "curse" // "denounce," not again found in parallelism, must be viewed in relation to the following bi-colon, the third couplet (Num. 23:8), containing the rhetorical question:

מה אקב לא קבה אל

ומה אזעם לא זעם יהוה

How shall I imprecate (whom) God hath not imprecated?
And how shall I denounce (whom) Yнwн hath not denounced?

The parallelism קבב // זעם, "imprecate" // "denounce," is found again in Prov. 24:24:

יקב -הו עמים

יזעמו -הו לאמים

Peoples shall *imprecate* him,
Populations shall *denounce* him.

Noting the sequence of the verbs "curse" // "denounce" (//) "imprecate" // "denounce," we may abstract the pattern of verb parallelism *a // b* (//) *c // b*, familiar from Isaac's blessing of Jacob (see pp. 43 f.).

IV

The sorcerer-poet proceeds in the fourth couplet to introduce a protasis, Num. 23:9*a*:

כי מראש צרים אראנו

ומגבעות אשורנו

When from the top of the crags I see him,
And from the hills I view him.

Isa. 38:11, Hab. 1:3 and 13, Ps. 10:14 and 84:10; and three times in reverse order but not in parallel: Hab. 1:5, Lam. 1:11 (=Lam. 2:20).

The remaining pair, "mischief" // "villainy," is also a traditional parallelism; cf. Isa. 10:1, Hab. 1:3, Ps. 7:15, Job 4:8 and 5:6. It also occurs in this order not in parallel: Ps. 55:11*b*; in reverse parallelism: Isa. 59:4*b*, Job 15:35; in reverse order not in parallel: Ps. 10:7 and 90:10.

[19] The parallelism "tent(s)" // "dwelling-place(s)" was traditional in Hebrew as in Ugaritic poetry (see Cassuto, *The Goddess Anath*, p. 26); cf. Isa. 54:2; Jer. 30:18; *UM* 128 III 18–19, 2 Aqht V 31–33. The pair occurs not in parallel in II Sam. 7:6 and I Chron. 17:5 and in reverse parallelism in Ps. 78:60.

Two sets of fixed pairs may be discerned here. The more easily recognized of the two is the parallelism of the verbs ראה // שור, "see" // "view," for, in addition to its employment here and in Balaam's fourth *mashal*, Num. 24:17a:

$$\text{א ר א נ ו ו ל א עתה}$$
$$\text{א ש ו ר נ ו ו ל א קרוב}$$

I *see* him but not now,
I *view* him, but not near,

it is found again in Job 35:5:

$$\text{הבט שמים ו-ר א ה}$$
$$\text{ו-ש ו ר שחקים גבהו ממך}$$

Look at heaven and *see*,
And *view* the clouds that are higher than thou,

and is probably to be noted in Job 7:7–8.

Most interesting from the point of view of the relation of biblical Hebrew to other West-Semitic dialects, and the dialectical relations of this particular poem, is the parallelism in this couplet of צרים // גבעות, "crags" // "hills." This particular pair does not again occur in the Old Testament. Rather, the regular parallelism in biblical Hebrew is (הר)ים // גבע)ות), "mountain(s)" // "hill(s)," for example Isa. 2:14:

$$\text{ועל כל ה-ה ר י ם הרמים}$$
$$\text{ועל כל ה-ג ב ע ו ת הנשאות}$$

And upon all the high *mountains*,
And upon all the lofty *hills*.

The pair occurs in this order thirty-one times,[20] in this order though not in parallelism eight times,[21] and three times in parallelism but in reverse order.[22] With so high a frequency of occurrence of the pair הר // גבע and with but one example of צר // גבע, one might well be tempted to emend צרים to הרים and so bring it into conformity with the rest of Hebrew poetic tradition. The finding in Ugaritic poetry six times of the fixed pair עֹר // גבע, however, renders the emendation highly improbable and clearly unnecessary;[23] note

[20] Gen. 49:26 (reading with Septuagint; cf. Hab. 3:6); Deut. 33:15; Isa. 2:2 and 14, 10:32, 30:17 and 25, 31:4, 40:12, 41:15, 54:10, 65:7; Jer. 4:24, 16:16, 50:6; Ezek. 34:6, 35:8; Hos. 4:13, 10:8; Joel 4:18; Amos 9:13; Mic. 4:1, 6:1; Nah. 1:5; Hab. 3:6; Ps. 72:3, 114:4 and 6; Prov. 8:25; Cant. 2:8, 4:6.

[21] Deut. 12:2; Isa. 40:4, 42:15, 55:12; Ezek. 6:3, 36:4 and 6; Ps. 148:9.

[22] Jer. 3:23, 17:2–3; Ezek. 6:13.

[23] Cf. Albright, *JBL* LXIII 212, n. 22.

UM 49 II 15–17:[24]

כל עָ ר לכבד אַרץ
כל ג ב ע לכבד שדמ

Every *crag* to the core of the earth,
Every *hill* to the core of the downs,

UM 51 V 77–78:[25]

תבלכ עָ ר מ מאָד כספ
ג ב ע מ מחמד חֹרצ

The *crags* shall bear thee much silver,
The *hills* an abundance(?) of gold,

UM ʿnt III 27–28:

בקדש ב-עָ ר נחלתי
בנעמ ב-ג ב ע תלאית

In the holy place, in the *crag* of my inheritance,
In the pleasant place, in the *hill* . . . ,

for Ugaritic ḡ is often represented in Hebrew cognates by צ. Compare, for example, Ugaritic יקḡ with Hebrew יקצ, Ugaritic נעָר with Hebrew נצר (Aramaic נטר), Ugaritic עָמא with Hebrew צמא. Ugaritic עָר, then (as Aramaic טור), has its cognate in Hebrew צר.[26] Since Balaam says he was brought by Balak from the "Mountains of Qedem," in all probability the mountains east of Byblos,[27] the use of the Syrian(?) parallelism צר // גבע rather than the Palestinian(?) parallelism הר // גבע would appear to indicate, on the one hand, an authentic representation of the northern dialect and, on the other hand, an accurate retention of the northern poetic tradition as it differed from the southern.

V

Having stated the protasis:

When from the top of the crags I see him (Israel),
And from the hills I view him,

[24] Cf. *UM* 67 VI 26–27.

[25] Cf. *UM* 51 V 93–94, 100–101.

[26] Cf. *inter alia*, Gordon, *UM*, pp. 23 f.; Albright, *JBL* LXIII 212, n. 22. But see also O. Rössler, *Zeitschrift für Assyriologie* LIV (1961) 165–67.

[27] Cf. Albright, *JBL* LXIII 211 f., n. 15; *idem*, *BASOR* No. 118 (1950) pp. 15 f., n. 13; A. S. Yehuda, *JBL* LXIV (1945) 547–51.

the poet in the apodosis, the fifth couplet, reports his finding, Num. 23:9*b:*

הן עם לבדד ישכן

ובגוים לא יתחשב(?)

Behold, a people dwelleth alone,
And among the nations doth not reckon itself(?).

The meaning of these words, as recognized by most commentators who point for confirmation to Jer. 49:31, is that the people, Israel, is safeguarded from harm—it is invulnerable.[28]

The first of the parallel pairs, עם // גוי , "people" // "nation(s)," is so regular and obvious a parallelism as hardly to require comment; note

Deut. 32:21*b:*

ואני אקניאם בלא ע ם

ב-ג ו י נבל אכעיסם

And I, I shall provoke them with a no *people,*
With a foolish *nation* I shall anger them,

II Sam. 22:44 (=Ps. 18:44):

ותפלטני מריבי ע מ י (ם

תשמרני לראש ג ו י ם

Thou hast delivered me from the strife of *peoples,*
Thou keepest me for a chief of *nations,*

Isa. 11:10:

עמד לנס ע מ י ם

אליו ג ו י ם ידרשו

He shall stand as an ensign of *peoples,*
Him shall *nations* seek.

The pair occurs more than twenty times in this sequence[29] and more than twenty times in reverse sequence.[30]

[28] G. B. Gray, *A Critical and Exegetical Commentary on the Book of Numbers,* p. 346; J. Mauchline in *Pres. Vol. to W. B. Stevenson,* p. 78; J. Marsh, *The Interpreter's Bible* II, commentary *ad loc.* For other views see A. F. von Gall in *Festgruss Bernhard Stade,* p. 25, and L. E. Binns, *The Book of Numbers,* p. 162, commentary *ad loc.*

[29] Deut. 32:21; II Sam. 22:44 (=Ps. 18:44); Isa. 11:10, 14:6, 25:3 and 7, 33:3; Jer. 6:22, 12:16–17, 27:13, 50:41; Mic. 4:1–2 and 3; Zeph. 2:9; Ps. 106:34–35. Cf. Deut. 4:6; II Sam. 7:23; Ezek. 28:25, 32:9; Hag. 2:14; Zach. 8:22; Jer. 33:24; Ps. 83:4–5, 106:4–5; Lam. 1:1.

[30] Deut. 32:8; Isa. 1:4, 2:2–3 and 4, 10:6, 18:2 (cf. 65:1–2), 30:28, 49:22, 61:9; Jer. 2:11; Ezek. 36:15; Mic. 5:7; Hab. 2:5 and 8; Ps. 33:10, 96:3 (=I Chron. 16:24), 105:13 (=I Chron. 16:20). Cf. also Gen. 17:16; Ezek. 25:7, 36:15; Zach. 2:15; Ps. 44:12–13, 47:9–10, 67:3–4, 96:10.

On the basis of this poet's adherence to an established tradition of fixed pairs of parallel words the received text of the second colon,

ובגוים לא יתחשב

And among the nations doth not reckon itself,

however conducive to impressive sermonizing, is most improbable. The verbal form יתחשב, *hitpaᶜᶜēl* of the root חשב, "to think," is a *hapax legomenon* in biblical Hebrew and, found only here, invites suspicion of the text. Moreover, while the verb in the first colon, שכן, never again appears in parallel with any form of the verb חשב, it is frequently found in parallel with the verbal root ישב, "to reside." Because we shall argue for an emendation of the text, all the available evidence is herewith presented,

Isa. 32:16:

ו-ש כ ן במדבר משפט

וצדקה בכרמל ת ש ב

Then shall justice *dwell* in the wilderness,
And righteousness *reside* in Carmel,

Isa. 33:24:

ובל יאמר ש כ ן חליתי

העם ה-י ש ב בה נשא עון

And no one who *dwelleth* (there) shall say, "I am ill"—
The people that *resideth* in it shall be forgiven (its) iniquity,

Jer. 17:6*b*:

ו-ש כ ן חררים במדבר

ארץ מלחה ולא ת ש ב

And he shall *dwell* in the parched places of the wilderness,
A salt land where none *resideth*,

Job 15:28*a*:

ו-י ש כ ו ן ערים נכחדות

בתים לא י ש ב ו למו

And he *dwelt* (in) desolated cities,
(In) houses (where) none *resideth*.

Note also the use of the parallelism in prose, I Kings 8:12*b*–13 (=II Chron. 6:1–2):

YHWH hath said he would *dwell* (ל-שכן) in thick darkness, I have indeed builded thee an exalted house, a place for thee to *reside* (ל-שבת-ך) forever.

In reverse sequence the parallelism is found in

Isa. 13:20a:

לא ת ש ב לנצח
ולא ת ש כ ן עד דור ודור

None shall *reside* (there) ever,
Nor *dwell* (there) for all generations,

Jer. 49:31:

קומו עלו אל גוי שליו י ו ש ב לבטח נאם יהוה
לא דלתים ולא בריח לו בדד י ש כ נ ו

"Arise! Go up against a nation at ease, *residing* secure," saith YHWH,
"Having no doors or bars, *dwelling* alone,"

Jer. 50:39b:

ולא ת ש ב עוד לנצח
ולא ת ש כ ו ן עד דור ודור

None shall *reside* (there) ever again,
Nor *dwell* (there) for all generations,

Ps. 68:17:

ההר חמד אלהים ל- ש ב ת -ו
אף יהוה י ש כ ן לנצח

. . . the mountain that God hath desired for his *residence*,
Even YHWH, (where) he *dwelleth* forever;

Job 29:25a:[31]

אבחר דרכם ו- א ש ב ראש
ו- א ש כ ו ן כמלך בגדוד

I would choose their way, and *reside* (as their) chief,
And would *dwell* as a king among (his) troop.

The uniqueness in biblical Hebrew of the form יתחשב and, indeed, of any form of the *hitpacēl* stem generally of this root, as well as the uniqueness of the parallelism of the verbs שכן // חשב, on the one hand, together with the overwhelming mass of evidence for a traditional parallelism of the verbs ישב // שכן, on the other hand, argues in the most convincing manner possible for the necessity to emend Massoretic יתחשב to a form of the verb ישב. The emendation nearest to hand, of course, is ייתשב; but, like the root חשב, the root ישב in the *hitpacēl* stem, known in post-biblical Hebrew, does not otherwise occur in biblical Hebrew. Emending יתחשב of the received text to יתישב would therefore be replacing one *hapax legomenon* for another. Of far greater im-

---

[31] Cf. also, perhaps, Isa. 26:18–19, Ob. 3, Zach. 8:3, Ps. 68:7, and the parallelism ŠKN // GWR // YŠB // ŠKN in Judg. 5:17.

portance, however, are the following considerations: (1) the evidence for the existence of a traditional parallelism of the terms בדד // בטח, "alone" // "secure," found in Deut. 33:28:[32]

וישכן ישראל ב ט ח

ב ד ד עין יעקב

And Israel dwelt *secure*,
Alone, the fount of Jacob;

(2) the existence of the combined parallelism בדד ישכנו // יושב לבטח found in Jer. 49:31 (for full citation of verse see above); and (3) the fact of the more than twenty occurrences of the phrase ישב (ל)בטח, "reside secure."[33] It is therefore highly probable that the text of the fifth couplet originally read:

הן עם לבדד ישכן

ובגוים ⸢לבטח ישב⸣

Behold, a people dwelleth alone,
And among the nations ⸢resideth secure⸣.

Its meaning would then be unequivocal: Balaam finds the people of Israel to be safe and secure—invulnerable to harm.

VI

The rhetorical question comprising the sixth couplet denies that anyone may hurt this people through magical means, Num 23:10a:

מי מנה עפר יעקב

ומ⟨י⟩ ספר את רבע ישראל

Who can count[34] the dust of Jacob?
And ⸢who can number⸣ the fourth part(?) of Israel?

To the regularity of the parallelism "Jacob" // "Israel" we have already called attention (pp. 52–55).

The correction in the second colon of the substantive מספר, "number," to ⟨מ⟩י ספר, "who can number," has been made by nearly all modern commentators,[35] for, in addition to the incomprehensibility of the verse as it stands, it

---

[32] Cf. Ps. 4:9.

[33] Lev. 25:18 and 19, 26:5; Deut. 12:10; Judg. 18:7; I Sam. 12:11; I Kings 5:5; Isa. 47:8; Jer. 32:37; Ezek. 28:26, 34:25 and 28, 38:8, 11, and 14, 39:6 and 26; Hos. 2:20; Zeph. 2:15; Zach. 14:11; Prov. 3:29.

[34] For such use of the perfect see Judg. 9:9 and 11 and cf. GKC, § 106 *n*, and S. R. Driver, *A Treatise on the Use of the Tenses in Hebrew* (2d ed.; Oxford, 1881) § 19.

[35] Albright, *JBL* LXIII 210, attributes the absence of the *yodh* to early orthography; G. R. Driver, "Abbreviations in the Massoretic Text," *Textus* I (1960) 123, suggests that the spelling without *yodh* is an abbreviation.

is dictated by two major factors: (1) the evidence of the Septuagint and Samaritan recensions and (2) the parallelism מנה // ספר , "count" // "number." These roots in parallel relation are found again in I Kings 3:8*b*:

עם רב אשר לא ימנה

ולא יספר מרב

A multitudinous people that cannot be *counted*,
And cannot be *numbered* for multitude.

In reverse sequence the pair occurs in I Kings 8:5 (= II Chron. 5:6):

אשר לא יספרו

ולא ימנו מרב

. . . that they could not be *numbered*,
and could not be *counted* for multitude,

as well as in Ugaritic, *UM* 77:45–47:[36]

הן בפי ספר -הן

בשפתי מנת -הן

Behold, in my mouth is their *number(ing)*,
On my lips their *count(ing)*.

Of more than passing interest is the use made of this pair in the twice-told promise of God to Abram concerning the latter's offspring (Gen. 13 and 15). In Gen. 13:16 we read:

And I shall make thy seed as the dust of the earth; which, if one be able to *count* (למנות) the dust of the earth, so too shall thy seed be *counted* (ימנה),

while in the parallel account, Gen. 15:5, there is found:

Look, prithee, heavenward and *number* (וספר) the stars—if thou be able to *number* (לספר) them.

That the appearance in these two parallel accounts of one member each of a fixed parallel pair is not fortuitous is more readily apparent when one notes in the same two accounts an identical application of the pair הבט // ראה, "look" // "see." (On the regularity of these verbs in parallel relationship in biblical Hebrew poetry see p. 54, n. 18.) Gen. 13:14 reads:

Raise thine eyes and *see* (וראה) . . . ,

while Gen. 15:5 has:

Look (הבט), prithee, heavenward. . . .

---

[36] Cf. Moshe Held, "Studies in Ugaritic Lexicography and Poetic Style" (unpublished Ph.D. dissertation, Johns Hopkins University, 1957; microfilm) p. 180.

Similar use is made of the pair מנה // ספר by the author of II Sam. 24:1–10, who writes of a census undertaken by David (verse 1):

And the anger of YHWH continued to kindle against Israel, and he instigated David against them, saying: "Go! *Count* (מנה) Israel and Judah!

At the conclusion of the census-taking we are told (verse 10):

And David's heart smote him after he had *numbered* (ספר) the people.

This technique of the Hebrew authors—employing each of the individual terms of a fixed parallel pair at each of the two extremes of a prose account—we shall have occasion to demonstrate yet again in the following study. Such use can owe its origin not to accident but only to art.

Supported by the evidence of the Greek and Samaritan versions, the emendation in our passage of מספר to ספר מ(י), which restores the parallelism of the verbs מנה // ספר, now seen to have been traditional, is thus virtually certain.

The remaining element in the second colon, את רבע, "the fourth part," is difficult because of the lack of a meaningful parallelism and the appearance of the accusative particle, את, in so early a poem. Emending the text to read רבבות, "ten-thousands," allegedly on the basis of the Septuagint, as most interpreters of the verse have done,[37] is inadmissible on several grounds: (1) עפר, "dust," is not otherwise found in parallel with רבבות, "ten-thousands"; (2) when רבבות appears in the second half of a bi-colon in Hebrew (as in Ugaritic) poetry, the fixed parallel in the first half is regularly אלפים, "thousands" (see pp. 16–17); (3) the Septuagint here has the parallelism σπέρμα // δήμους, "seed" // "peoples," neither element of which is reflected in the Massoretic text; and (4) the regular rendering of Hebrew רבבות in the Septuagint is μυριάς, "myriad," and not δῆμος, "people."

The apparently correct solution to the textual problem, which does not seem to have gained universal acceptance, was first proffered by Friedrich Delitzsch, who suggested—calling attention to our verse—a comparison with Akkadian *turbuʾ(tu)*, "dust cloud."[38] This found endorsement by such eminent scholars as Frants Buhl,[39] H. L. Ginsberg,[40] B. Landsberger,[41] and W. F. Al-

[37] G. B. Gray, *A Critical and Exegetical Commentary on the Book of Numbers*, p. 347; A. F. von Gall in *Festgruss Bernhard Stade*, p. 25; L. E. Binns, *The Book of Numbers*, p. 162, commentary *ad loc.*; S. Mowinckel, *ZAW* XLVIII (1930) 262 f., n. 2; J. Marsh, *The Interpreter's Bible* II 255, commentary *ad loc.*

[38] F. Delitzsch, *Assyrische Lesestücke* (4te Aufl.; Leipzig, 1900) p. 184 *b*.

[39] In *Wilhelm Gesenius' Hebräisches und aramäisches Handwörterbuch über das Alte Testament* (14th ed.; Leipzig, 1905) p. 678 *a* (cf. also 15th ed. [1910], p. 736 *b*).

[40] *ZAW* LI (1933) 309.

[41] *Die Fauna des alten Mesopotamien nach der 14. Tafel der Serie ḪAR-ra = Ḫubullu* (Leipzig, 1934) p. 123, n. 3.

bright.[42] The emendation thus advanced is most attractive in that the necessary alteration of the text is slight and the resulting parallelism is both meaningful and appropriate. Furthermore, Albright recognized in the "un-Assyrian form" *turbuʾtu* an Aramaic loan-word from an as yet unattested **tarbuʿtu*. This is confirmed by the spelling *ta-ar-bu-úḫ-tum* in a lexical text.[43] With the scholars enumerated above we may unhesitatingly adopt the reading **tarbuʿat*, assigning it a meaning "raised dust" or the like, and render our passage:

מי מנה עפר יעקב

ומ'י' ספר (א)(תרבע(ת) ישראל

Who can count the dust of Jacob?
And ⸢who can number⸣ ⸢the (raised) dust⸣ of Israel?

The rhetorical nature of the question is obvious. Not so obvious, however, is its significance. Almost all who have dealt with the text have seen in the question an allusion to the numerical strength of the people of Israel. Not unnaturally, attention has been drawn to the promises of God to Abram and to Jacob, promises of a posterity as innumerable as the dust of the earth (Gen. 13:16, 28:14).[44] What has been overlooked in these comparisons, however, is that, while God's promises involve the figure of counting—or rather the impossibility of counting—dust, it is the dust of the earth that is innumerable; that is to say, an analogy is there drawn between the uncountable particles of the earth's dust and the envisioned number of the patriarch's descendants. In our text, however, the poet speaks of the counting of the dust of "Jacob" // "Israel," not the dust of the earth and not the numbers of the people. Moreover, the context of the sixth couplet demands that Balaam's question—as, indeed, his entire poem—comment upon the impossibility of harming Israel by (any form of) enchantment. The sorcerer-poet has already stated, in the third couplet, his own limitations: he cannot curse if God has not cursed. Since the fourth and fifth couplets together declare emphatically the safety and security—the virtual impregnability—of Israel, the sixth couplet cannot refer to the numbers of this people (which is meaningless in the context), but can only refer to the futility of anyone's attempting to injure it, as he (Balaam) has been called upon to do through sorcery. The expression "to count/number the dust of someone," in turn, must denote a practice, not otherwise known in biblical literature, having magical significance.

In Akkadian incantation literature, where complaint is often registered

---

[42] *JBL* LXIII 213, n. 28.

[43] Ea IV 86; cited in *CAD* IV 184 *b* (under *eperu*, lex. section).

[44] See e.g. G. B. Gray, *A Critical and Exegetical Commentary on the Book of Numbers*, p. 347.

against those responsible for the supplicant's discomfort, the ones held responsible are called "wizard" and "witch" and are accused of having performed magical rites which have brought about the suffering of the complainant. Among the rites enumerated is that of collecting(?) or gathering(?) up dust of the victim's feet. In one case the sorcerer, it is suggested, has placed this material in a grave.[45] That the manipulation of the dust of the feet was held to be a relatively regular and commonplace activity for practitioners of "black magic" in ancient Mesopotamia is distinctly intimated by the frequency with which it is mentioned,[46] for example *BMS*, No. 12, line 55:

SAḪAR (*epir*) GÌR^{II}.MU (*šēpē-ia$_5$*) *šab-su*
min-da-ti-ia$_5$ li-qa

The dust of my feet has been collected,
My measurements have been taken,[47]

and *AOF* XVIII 291, line 21:

SAḪAR (*epir*) GÌR^{II}.MU (*šēpē-ia$_5$*) *iš-bu-šu*
man-da-at la-ni-ia$_5$ ú-man-di-du

They have gathered up the dust of my feet,
They have taken the measurements of my body.

The meaning, then, of Balaam's sixth couplet, the rhetorical question:

Who can count the dust of Jacob?
And ⌜who can number⌝ ⌜the (raised) dust⌝ of Israel?

would appear to be: "Who can bewitch Israel?"

TRANSLATION OF THE RECONSTRUCTED TEXT

From Aram did Balak fetch me,
The king of Moab from the Mountains of Qedem.

Go! Curse for me Jacob!
And go! Denounce Israel!

How shall I imprecate (whom) God hath not imprecated?
And how shall I denounce (whom) Yнwн hath not denounced?

When from the top of the crags I see him,
And from the hills I view him—

---

[45] *Keilschrifttexte aus Assur religiösen Inhalts I* ("Wissenschaftliche Veröffentlichung der Deutsche Orient-Gesellschaft" XXVIII [Leipzig, 1919]) No. 80:30 f., duplicate in *RA* XXVI (1929) 40:19 f. (cited in *CAD* IV 185 *b*).

[46] *CAD* IV 185 *b* lists seven examples, and another has since been published by W. G. Lambert, "An Incantation of the Maqlû Type," *AOF* XVIII (1960) 291, line 21. [I am indebted for knowledge of Lambert's study to Prof. E. Reiner.]

[47] The translation is that of *CAD* IV 185 *b*.

Behold, a people dwelleth alone,
And among the nations resideth secure!

Who can count the dust of Jacob?
And who can number the (raised) dust of Israel?

. . . .
. . . .[48]

ADDITIONAL NOTE ON THE PARALLELISM קרקר // פאתי
(NUM. 24:17*b*)

This half-verse in Balaam's fourth *mashal*, beginning:

A star shall arise out of Jacob . . . ,

is of interest not only because of the possible (if improbable) allusion to a messianic age but also because of an apparent textual difficulty in the latter part of it. The difficulty is more apparent than real, however, and close scrutiny of the text reveals the necessity to recognize a term hitherto unknown in biblical Hebrew, though having cognates in Akkadian and in post-biblical Hebrew. That portion of the verse with which we are concerned reads:

ומחץ פאתי מואב
וקרקר כל בני שת

And it shall smite . . . of Moab,
And . . . all the B^enê Shêth.

With the exception of the Samaritan and one Greek recension to be noted below (p. 70), the ancient versions are unanimous in understanding פאתי to be the parallel of בני and in reading קרקר as a verb.

Targum Onkelos:

And he shall kill the chiefs (רברבי) of Moab,
And shall rule over (ישלוט) the sons of man;

Septuagint:

And he shall crush the princes (ἀρχηγοὺς) of Moab,
And shall plunder (προνομεύσει) all the sons of Seth;

Vulgate:

And shall strike all the chiefs (*duces*) of Moab,
And shall waste (*vastabitque*) all the children of Seth;

[48] In its present form the seventh couplet is unintelligible to me. I would suggest as an initial step toward a possible reconstruction or understanding of the text the association in parallel cola of YŠR // ʾḤRYT; cf. e.g. Ps. 37:37. In addition, attention may be drawn to the parallelism occurring in Ugaritic, ʾuḥryt // ʾaṯryt, on which see the remarks of Ginsberg in *BASOR* No. 98 (1945) pp. 21 f. and the writer's observations in *VT* XI (1961) 147, n. 6, and 148, n. 3.

Peshitta:

> And shall destroy the heroes (ﻟﺒﺼ) of Moab,
> And subdue (ﻟﻤﺼ) all the *Bny Šyt*.

Alone among the ancient versions the Samaritan text instead of קרקר reads קדקד, "pate," but is otherwise in strict agreement with the Massoretic text. This reading of the Samaritan recension has found favor with virtually all modern commentators, who point to the text of Jer. 48:45 for confirmation of their proposed emendation of קרקר to קדקד:

ותאכל פאת מואב

וקדקד בני שאון

> And it (the fire) shall consume the . . . of Moab,
> And the pate of the Bᵉnê Shāᵒôn.

The choice, plainly, lies between seeing in קרקר a verb, in which case the parallelism would be מחץ // קרקר, or a noun, in which case the parallelism is פאת(י) // קרקר (קדקד). Whichever the choice, the two texts (Num. 24:17b and Jer. 48:45) must be compared and their parallelisms at least must be brought into agreement. That is to say, either קרקר or קדקד must be corrected. Support for the existence of a verb, קרקר, might perhaps be sought in Isa. 22:5, but this text is so filled with uncertainties as to be of little value for elucidation of the passage in Balaam's *mashal*. Furthermore, two observations argue against the form in question being a verb: (1) we should expect the vocalization *qirqēr* (as in post-biblical Hebrew and as in the reduplicated forms *gilgēl, ṭilṭēl, kilkēl*, and post-biblical Hebrew *hirhēr*) rather than *qarqar*; (2) the meaning assigned to this problematic verb, "break down," ill suits the activity of its subject, "fire," in the Jeremiah reference. I am inclined, therefore, with most modern commentators and against the evidence of the versions cited above, to see in the word under discussion a noun and not a verb. If it be ruled out as a verb, as in these two texts I think it must, the question that remains is whether Num. 24:17b or Jer. 48:45 has preserved the correct reading and, accordingly, whether קרקר of Balaam's *mashal* or קדקד of Jeremiah's prophecy is to be emended so as to be brought into agreement with a traditional פאה // קרקר (קדקד) parallelism.

Along with the acceptance of the superiority of the Jeremiah text has gone the rendering of פאת מואב as "the temple (forehead) of Moab," this clearly and only because of the apparent parallelism with קדקד. Yet the basic meaning of Hebrew פאה is "edge," "border," "side," in which it agrees with its Akkadian and Ugaritic cognates.[49] Nevertheless, it has been assumed that in

---

[49] The parallelism *pnm // pᵒi[t]*, occurring once in Ugaritic, would seem to constitute a cogent argument for those who would see in the latter word a term for a part of the face. But

biblical Hebrew the term has taken on the more specific meaning of "side of the head," "temple." In the sole example where פאה may with certainty be rendered "temple" it is in construct relation with "head," Lev. 19:27: "you shall not round off the side of your head (פאת ראשכם)," that is, "your temple." It may also perhaps have the same meaning when found in construct

---

rendering this parallelism as "face" // "forehead (brow)" is conjectural at best. The verse in its entirety (*UM* 2 Aqht II 8–9) reads:

ב-ד-!נא[ו]ל] פנם תשמֹח

ו-על יצהל פא[ת]

and has been translated by Ginsberg (*ANET*, p. 150) thus:

Daniel's face lights up,
While above his forehead shines,

an interpretation based at least in part on Ps. 104:15:

וײן ישמח לבב אנוש

להצהיל פנים משמן

ולחם לבב אנוש יסעד

But a problem clearly revolves around the meaning of the root ṢHL, which, outside this one occurrence, always and regularly in biblical Hebrew means "to make a noise" (usually of joy, rarely of sorrow, and often used to denote the neighing of a horse), particularly when it occurs, as here, in association with ŚMḤ. Cf. Jer. 31:7a:

רנו ליעקב שמחה

וצהלו בראש הגוים

Shout for Jacob with joy!
And make a noise for the chief of nations!

and Esther 8:15b (cf. also Jer. 50:11):

והעיר שושן צהלה ושמחה

And the city Shushan made noise and rejoiced.

It is therefore at least questionable whether ṢHL is to be rendered "to shine." Moreover, the appearance in Ugaritic of the phrase g/ṣ!hl ph (*UM* 8:3) suggests that the Ugaritic passage in question (*UM* 2 Aqht II 8–9) may have to be read (cf. Gordon, *UM*, § 20:1616) and translated:

ב-ד-!נא[ו]ל] פנם תשמֹח

ו-על יצהל פה!

Danil's face (inner part?) rejoiceth,
While above, his mouth maketh (joyful) noise.

Cf. *ēliš ina šaptēšu itammâ ṭubbāti* // *šaplānu libbašu kaṣir nīrtu,* "above with his lips he speaks amities // below, his heart is fastened on murder" (M. Streck, *Assurbanipal* [Leipzig, 1916] II 28 iii 80–81).

relation with "face" (as in Lev. 13:41), פְּאַת פָּנָיו, "the side of his face," and
in the expression פְּאַת זָקָן, "the edge of the beard" (Lev. 19:27, 21:5)—but
nowhere else with any degree of certainty.[50]

Three times, all in the Book of Jeremiah, appears the construct chain קְצוּצֵי
פֵאָה, which with rare exceptions has been understood to mean "those who
cut the corner(s) of their hair."[51] The contexts of all three occurrences, however, suggest quite a different understanding. In the first of the passages (Jer.
9:25) the prophet pronounces divine punishment:

> . . . on Egypt, and on Judah, and on Edom, and on the Ammonites, and on Moab,
> and on all קְצוּצֵי פֵאָה, those who reside in the desert.

In the second passage (Jer. 25:18–26), the prophet lists those peoples to
whom YHWH has sent him in order to have them "drink from the cup" he
has received from YHWH's hand:

> Jerusalem and the cities of Judah, its kings and princes, . . . Pharaoh, king of Egypt,
> and his servants, and his princes, and all his people, and all the foreign folk(?), and all
> the kings of the land of Uz, and all the kings of the land of the Philistines, and Ashke-
> lon, and Gaza, and Ekron, and the remnant of Ashdod; Edom, and Moab, and the
> Ammonites; and all the kings of Tyre, and all the kings of Sidon, and the kings of the
> coast-land which is across the sea; and Dedan, and Tema, and Buz, and all קְצוּצֵי פֵאָה;
> and all the kings of Arabia; and all the kings of ʿEreb(?), who dwell in the desert; and
> all the kings of Zimri, and all the kings of Elam, and all the kings of Madai. . . .

It is clear from these passages that the lists are geographically oriented. The
expression קְצוּצֵי פֵאָה, therefore, must also refer to the geographic location of
people and not to some distinctive coiffure. In so far as this designation is preceded by names of settled peoples and regions and followed by reference to
"those who dwell/reside in the desert," קְצוּצֵי פֵאָה must signify those groups
that live between the settled and the unsettled regions, between "the desert
and the sown," that is to say, on the marginal lands, and therefore is to be
rendered "frontiersmen" or the like (lit.: "those who are limited with respect
to the frontier"). In the third passage (Jer. 49:31–32) the קְצוּצֵי פֵאָה are said
to have "no doors or bars," that is to say, no permanent habitations, but to
keep camels and cattle, a very adequate description of those seminomadic

[50] It seems to me rash and unprofitable to appeal to Isa. 3:17, where it would be necessary
to emend פתהן to פ(א)תהן in order to obtain a parallelism קדקד // פֵאָה, for not only
would the assertion be based on a problematic emendation but the reversal in sequence would
require explanation. As has long been suggested, it is likely that Hebrew PT(HN) of Isa. 3:17
is to be equated with Akkadian *pūtu*, "brow."

[51] Lit.: "those who are cut off with respect to the side." For similar constructions cf.
קְרֻעֵי בְגָדִים (II Sam. 13:31, Jer. 41:5) and נְטִילֵי כָסֶף (Zeph. 1:11) and see *GKC*,
§ 116 *k*.

groups that range the fringes of the desert.[52] The term פאה is thus seen consistently to have retained its meaning "edge," "border," "frontier," and the like and never independently to mean "temple(s)."

Furthermore, it must be borne in mind, the two texts in question witness to a unique use in biblical Hebrew of פאה in construct relationship with a territorial designation, "Moab." While it may, perhaps, be compared with biblical Hebrew פאת שדך, "the edge of thy field,"[53] and Ugaritic פאת מדבר, "the edge of the desert,"[54] a more exact comparison is to be found in an Akkadian text from Mari in which reference is made to an encampment (nawûm) said to be located i-na pi-e-at Za-al-ma-a-qi-im[KI], "on the frontier of (the country) Zalmāqum."[55] At this point we may introduce the evidence of the Greek version Symmachus, wherein ומחץ פאתי מואב of Num. 24:17 is rendered καὶ παίσει κλίματα Μωάβ, "and it shall strike the regions of Moab." There is no reason, therefore, beyond the desire to see in פאת(י) מואב a parallelism of קדקד, to translate "the forehead / temple(s) of Moab"; rather must it—and, indeed, can it only—be rendered "the border(s)/frontier(s) of Moab."[56]

[52] After having completed the above argument on the meaning of פאה קצוצי, I was pleased to learn that I had been anticipated in this interpretation by the eleventh-century commentator Rashi, who explained the phrase in Jer. 9:25 as "those set apart on the edge of the desert," המוקצין בפאת מדבר. Cf. also D. Qimḥi in his commentary on Jer. 25:23.

[53] Lev. 19:9 and 23:22.

[54] UM 52:68, 75 I 35, Krt 105 and 193–94.   [55] ARM II 35:7–8.

[56] It might perhaps be objected that the verb mḥṣ in biblical Hebrew takes as its object "head" (Hab. 3:13; Ps. 68:22, 110:6), "loins" (Deut. 33:11), "kings" (Ps. 110:5), and "Rahab" (Job 26:12) but never a (section of a) land or country. That it is not otherwise attested need carry no undue weight in the argument, however. Note that in Old Akkadian and in the texts from Mari and Alalakh, just as in biblical Hebrew, the verb maḫāṣu takes as its object "head" (contra Moshe Held in JAOS LXXIX [1959] 170). Old Akkadian evidence is provided by i-na ti-ir-ti ᵈKA.DI be-li-šu qá-qá-ad um-ma-nim [š]i-a-ti im-ḫa-ṣú-na, "at the command of (the god) Sataran, his lord, he smote the head of that army" (Louis Speleers, Recueil des inscriptions de l'Asie Antérieure des Musées royaux du Cinquantenaire à Bruxelles [Bruxelles, 1925] No. 4, rev. 1–7), and Ilumutabil, the viceroy (šakanakkum) of Dêr, is called ma-ḫi-iṣ qá-qá-ad um-ma-an An-ša-an[KI] NIM-tim Ši-maš[KI]-im, "the one who smites the head of the army of Anshan, Elam, and Shimashum" (Cuneiform Texts from Babylonian Tablets, &c., in the British Museum XXI [London, 1905] Pl. 1, No. 91084, lines 10–14). At Mari the expression māḫiṣ qaqqadim, "smiter of the head," occurs in the sense of "accuser," ma-ḫi-iṣ qa-qa-di-šu-nu (Symb. Kosch. p. 113, lines 15, 22 f., 27; cf. D. J. Wiseman, The Alalakh Tablets [London, 1953] Text No. *11, lines 20–21). Significantly, at Mari there are found aš-šum ḫa-ṣi-ra-tim ù rubṣātim(?)ḪI.A ša Ḫa-na-a DUMU.MEŠ Ia-mi-im ma-ḫa-ṣi-im . . . be-li ú-wa-er-an-ni, "my lord has given command to smite the sheepfolds and cattle-folds(?) of the Hanean Yaminites" (Mél. Dussaud II 989 c 4–6), and iš-tu u₄-mi-im ša be-li i-na na-wi-e DUMU.MEŠ Ia-mi-in im-ḫa-ṣu, "from the day that my lord smote the encampments of the Yaminites . . ." (Mél. Dussaud II 992 c 8'–11'). Most significant of all perhaps is the text ARM I 123. In this letter Ishme-Dagan informs his brother that the ruler of Eshnunna is determined to conquer the city Mulhanum. "And I," he writes, "shall I (but) mark it? I shall smite his country in retaliation" (pu-ḫa-am a-na ma-a-ti-šu a-ma-aḫ-ḫa-aṣ)! Cf. CAD IV 202.

Turning our attention now to the second half of the parallel pair, we note that קרקר as a common noun is a *hapax legomenon* in biblical Hebrew. Our investigation, accordingly, must begin with the remaining possibility, קדקד. When קדקד, "pate," as here, is the second term of a parallel pair, the first term is generally found to be ראש, "head," both in Old Testament and in Ugaritic poetry (see pp. 7–8). Were the emendation in Balaam's poem of קרקר to קדקד to be adopted, it would suggest very strongly the additional correction of פאת(י) to ראש(י)—an emendation not too farfetched in the light of the renderings of the versions cited on pages 66 f. but highly unlikely in view of its twofold occurrence as the first of the parallel pair. (To say nothing of the orthographic difficulties involved!) The remaining alternative, therefore, is to see in קדקד of the Jeremiah text an error for קרקר and to seek a definition of the latter term.

The passage itself suggests a definition. The fire, proceeding from the city Heshbon, is said to have "consumed the *frontier* of Moab." The parallel term קרקר, then, must signify some aspect of the *territory* "of the Benê Šāʾôn." Now, just as in Hebrew the reduplicated form *dardar*, "thorn," finds its cognate in Akkadian *daddaru*, "a thorny plant," Hebrew (and Ugaritic) *qodqōd*, "pate," in Akkadian *qaqqadu*, "head," West-Semitic *kabkab*, "star," in Akkadian *kakkabu*, "star," etc., so might we legitimately expect Hebrew *qarqar* to find its cognate in Akkadian *qaqqaru*. This term is common in Akkadian and has the meaning "ground," "territory." While such definition is adequate for both biblical contexts, since post-biblical Hebrew preserves a feminine form of this noun, namely קרקרה, to which have been assigned the meanings "the rimmed bottom of a vessel" and "the lower border of a net"[57]—the basic meaning of which must be "rim" or "border"—we, accordingly, may suggest for the masculine form of this noun in biblical Hebrew the meaning "(border)land." This definition of קרקר suits admirably both the text of Jeremiah and that of Balaam, the latter of which may therefore be rendered:

> And it shall smite the frontiers of Moab,
> And the (border)land of all the Benê Sheth,

and should prove not too far wrong.

[57] Jastrow, *Dictionary* II 1427 *a*.

STUDY V

DAVID'S LAMENT OVER SAUL AND JONATHAN[1]

The rite of the lament is a necessary and an only possible human countermeasure against the loss incurred by death. In the lament, through the intensification to the highest point of the emotional ties with the departed, his unity with the community is emotionally asserted in the face of the powers that separate, and the separation is overcome—insofar as possible—through the vividness of the recall and the nearness and presence of the departed in the spirit and the heart of the mourners. And at the same time this emphasizing of emotional ties is a pacification and an act of love toward the departed. . . .[2]

PROFESSOR JACOBSEN's incisive appraisal of the significance of lamentation may serve as an over-all and general introduction for us in our attempts at understanding the present text; for the dirge is David's response to the news of the death in battle of his one-time king, Saul, and of Saul's son, his friend Jonathan. It is furthermore the lament of a man of war for men of war and embodies his awareness of, and profound admiration for, their skill and achievements.

In addition, the lamentation is David's *poetic* response to these deaths. We emphasize this aspect because, however charged with emotion, however moving, it is not simply an uncontrolled or unstructured outpouring of grief.[3] The lament was a recognized literary genre in David's day, having had a venerable tradition in the ancient Near East,[4] and we must be prepared, therefore, to find his elegy stylistically conditioned by his poetic art.

[1] II Sam. 1:18–27.

[2] Thorkild Jacobsen, "Toward the Image of Tammuz," *History of Religions* I (1962) 201 f.

[3] Cf. e.g. David's oral response to the news of the death of his son Absalom (II Sam. 19:1).

[4] Examples are extant from Mesopotamian and Syrian as well as from biblical sources. These fall readily into two categories: (1) those that lament the destruction of cities or regions and (2) those that lament the death of individuals, whether divine, semidivine, or human. For the first category see "Lamentation over the Destruction of Ur," translated by S. N. Kramer in *ANET*, pp. 455–63; Ezek. 26:17–18, 27:2–36; Amos 5:2; and, the parade example in the Bible, the Book of Lamentations. Cf. further Jer. 9:9–11. For a selection of texts of the second category from Mesopotamia see Jacobsen, *History of Religions* I 189–213; for Syrian laments see the Ugaritic texts *UM* 62:6–7, and 67 VI 23–24 (translation in *ANET*, p. 139), *UM* 125:1–11, 14–23, and 98–111 (translation *ibid.* pp. 147–48). Cf. also, perhaps, Bion's *Lament for Adonis*. For biblical laments over individuals, other than that under discussion, see II Sam. 3:33–34, I Kings 13:29–30, Jer. 22:18 and 34:5, Ezek. 28:12–19 and 32:2–8.

Moreover, it may perhaps be hazarded, for the deaths that he here bewails David may have felt at least in part responsible. It was in the service of Saul that David had risen to prominence as a military leader, gained the love of Saul's daughter, Michal, and her hand in marriage, becoming son-in-law to the king, and won the selfless friendship of Jonathan, the heir apparent, who risked the violence of his father's anger—and therein his very life—defending David. Then, hunted as an outlaw leader of an outlaw band, David sought and gained service with Achish, the Philistine king of Gath. Sometime after, in concert with the other four Philistine rulers, Achish joined battle with the Israelite forces in the fateful encounter at Gilboa in which Saul and Jonathan lost their lives. Though he was excused from participating in this engagement, one may wonder, on the basis of his avowed willingness to fight on the Philistine side against Israel and his failure to come to the sorely needed help of those to whom he owed so much, whether David is not "overcompensating" in his lament for a guilty conscience.[5] However this may be, and however poor the state of the text's repair, David's poem must be recognized for what it is: a genuine expression of deep sorrow and a masterpiece of early Hebrew poetry.

I

The lamentation is introduced with the words:

And David keened this keening over Saul and over Jonathan his son. And he said . . . .

It is generally recognized that what follows, however unintelligible the received text may at present appear, must have constituted in its original form the opening lines of the dirge.[6] As these stand, however,

ללמד בני יהודה קשת

הנה כתובה על ספר הישר

they can only be rendered:

> To teach the sons of Judah (a/the) bow;
> Behold, it is inscribed in the Book of the Upright.

Each of the terms is perfectly plain and unambiguous, yet the obscurity and confusion created by their particular association are irritatingly obvious.[7] Since the versions reflect a text essentially similar to this, they afford no independent

[5] Cf. Jacobsen's suggestion of the possible element of guilt in the laments for "Dumuzi of the Grain" (*History of Religions* I 201 f.).

[6] Cf. II Sam. 3:33.

[7] For a clear statement of the difficulties and absurdities attendant on this (necessary) translation, see H. P. Smith, *A Critical and Exegetical Commentary on the Books of Samuel*, pp. 259 f.

help beyond the indication that whatever corruptions have entered were already present at the time of the text's translation into Greek, Aramaic, and Latin. Whoever, therefore, would make a serious attempt at elucidating the passage must, of necessity, resort to conjectural emendation.

One such emendation, which has received widespread acceptance and is eminently attractive, is that of H. P. Smith,[8] who suggested seeing in the words בני יהודה, "(the) sons of Judah," a corruption of בכי יהודה, "weep O Judah!" In this way an entirely apt summons is achieved by a relatively simple correction. Unfortunately, Smith went little farther, considering the remainder of the verse a later, explanatory addition, and sought the parallel clause to his reconstruction in the following verse. If the restoration "weep O Judah" is sound and represents, as I suppose, the original text, we should expect to find among the following phrases an appropriate echo, another call to mourning, whose component members balance with poetic precision the two elements "weep" and "Judah." As a parallel to the latter term we should expect "Israel," as in

Jer. 23:6a:

בימיו תושע יהודה
ו-ישראל ישכן לבטח

In his days Judah shall be saved,
And Israel shall dwell secure,

Hos. 2:2aα:

ונקבצו בני יהודה
ובני ישראל יחדו

And the Children of Judah shall be gathered,
And the Children of Israel together,

Ps. 114:2:

היתה יהודה לקדשו
ישראל ממשלותיו

Judah became his holy (place),
Israel his dominion.

As a parallel to the term "weep" we should expect "mourn," "wail," or the like. Now a not infrequent pair, of which בכה is one member, is בכה // ספד, "weep" // "mourn," found, for example, in Eccl. 3:4:

עת לבכות ועת לשחק
עת ספוד ועת רקוד

A time to weep, and a time to play,
A time to mourn, and a time to dance,

[8] *Ibid.* p. 260.

and both members of this pair occur in close association in

Gen. 23:2*b*:

ויבא אברהם לספד לשרה ו-לבכתה

And Abraham went in to *mourn* for Sarah and to (be)*weep* her,

II Sam. 1:12:[9]

ו-יספדו ו-יבכו

And they *mourned* and they *wept*,

Ezek. 24:16:[10]

ולא תספד ולא תבכה

And thou shalt not *mourn*, neither shalt thou *weep*.

Furthermore, this pair in derived forms occurs in Ugaritic verse, *UM* 1 Aqht 171–72:[11]

ערב בכית בהכלה

משספדת בחטֹרה

(Women) *weepers* enter into his palace,
(Women) *mourners* into his court,

and, interestingly enough, in an inscription of Ashurbanipal written in Akkadian:[12]

i-bak-ku-ú ᴸᵘSIPA.MEŠ ᴸᵘ*na-qí-di šá* la ab bi ik [. . .]
i-sa-ap-pi-du da-ad-me ur-ru u mu-šú [. . .]

The shepherds (and) herders *weep* . . .
The dwellings *mourn* day and night.

To the extent that our evidence permits, we may regard ספד // בכה as a traditional set of parallel terms; and, having reconstructed the existence of the first of them, we may allow ourselves the opportunity to search out and to find whether the second may not be hidden, camouflaged by the unintelligible jumble of this first verse. Its outline is clearly visible, I submit, in the problematic ספר הישר, "the Book of the Upright," whose very existence has been seriously doubted.[13] The emendation necessary to alter ספר into the suggested ספד is of the simplest kind, while emending ישר to read ישראל is not, perhaps,

---

[9] Cf. further II Sam. 3:31 f., Isa. 22:12, Esther 4:3.

[10] Cf. Ezek. 24:23.

[11] Cf. *UM* 1 Aqht 182–84.

[12] S. A. Smith, *Die Keilschrifttexte Asurbanipals* II (Leipzig, 1887) text K 2867 and p. 2, lines 30–31. Cf. Streck, *Assurbanipal* II, Ann. 11, rev. 10–11 (p. 215).

[13] Cf. James A. Montgomery, *A Critical and Exegetical Commentary on the Books of Kings* ("International Critical Commentary" [Edinburgh, 1951]) p. 192.

without precedent.[14] The parallelism would then appear to have been:

בכי יהודה

ספד ישראל

Weep O Judah!
Mourn O Israel!

When these phrases are so isolated and set in parallel structure, the remaining words of the verse, for the most part, fall readily into place, while the problems and their solutions assume a correspondingly greater measure of clarity. Thus, since "mourn O Israel" ends the second colon, it is highly probable that "weep O Judah" ends the first, so that the enigmatic קשת is to be joined with what follows in the second colon rather than with "weep O Judah," which precedes. It is then furthermore likely that קשת is to be read, not with the vocalization of the Massoretic text as קָשֶׁת (pausal form of קֶשֶׁת), "bow," but as קְשַׁת, construct form of the adjective קָשֶׁה, "hard," "severe," and the like, as in קְשַׁת רוּחַ (I Sam. 1:15). This suggests that its parallel in the first colon, which of a certainty must be sought in the form ללמד, is to be found in the latter half of it: מד, a simple error for מר, the adjective "bitter." The noun modified by "bitter," the remnant of which is לל, it may be supposed, was originally ילל, "wail(ing),"[15] and the entire expression ילל מר, "a bitter wailing," may be compared with מספד מר, "a bitter mourning" (Ezek. 27:31). What remains, then, is to identify in the words הנה כתובה על and, more specifically in the first of these, הנה, the noun with which קשת was in construct relationship and which, together with it, served as the parallel to ילל מר. This, I suppose, was the term נהי, "lament(ation)," the construct chain קשת נהי being rendered "grievous lament."[16]

Still unaccounted for are the words כתובה על, "inscribed upon," which, lacking all context, must be regarded as an explanatory addition inserted, once the corruption of the text had gotten under way, in a last desperate attempt to give some order to what by that time had developed into hopeless chaos.

The text of the initial lines of the lamentation thus reconstructed will have read:

ילל מר בכי יהודה

קשת נהי ספד ישראל

(With) a bitter wailing, weep O Judah!
(With) a grievous lament, mourn O Israel!

[14] Cf. G. R. Driver in *Textus* I 114.

[15] Cf. Deut. 32:10, on which see S. R. Driver, *A Critical and Exegetical Commentary on Deuteronomy* ("International Critical Commentary" [New York, 1895]) p. 357.

[16] It may be remarked that all these (reconstructed) terms are frequently found associated in varying combinations. Cf. e.g. Jer. 31:15, Joel 1:5, Mic. 1:8, etc.

II

הצבי ישראל על במותיך חלל

איך נפלו גבורים

Some of the difficulties inherent in the second verse are evident in the various attempts at translating it into English, for example

King James Version:

> The beauty of Israel is slain upon thy high places:
> How are the mighty fallen!

American Standard Revised and Revised Standard Versions:

> Thy glory, O Israel, is slain upon thy high places!
> How are the mighty fallen!

American Translation:

> Thy beauty, O Israel!
> Upon thy heights is slain.
> How have the heroes fallen.

Since the first term, according to the received text, bears the definite article it cannot be construed as standing in construct relation with the second,[17] and these cannot therefore be rendered with the King James Version "the beauty *of* Israel." And in the absence of the pronominal suffix neither can they be rendered with the other versions quoted above "*thy* glory, O Israel" or "*thy* beauty, O Israel." Moreover, the suitability of the term "beauty" or "glory" (lit.: *gazelle*) to denote Saul and/or Jonathan has been justly doubted.[18]

The problems, unfortunately, do not end there. The translation of במותיך as "thy high places," though never questioned, is not easily defended. For if, as must be assumed, by the term "high places"—plural of one of the technical terms for "place of worship"[19]—is meant Gilboa, then we must remind ourselves that Gilboa is not otherwise known to have been (in this sense) a "high place" or "high places." In addition, the pronominal suffix "*thy* (high places)" can refer only to Israel. And for anyone, but particularly for David, to designate Gilboa as Israel's high place(s) at a time immediately following the disastrous Battle of Gilboa, in which Saul and his sons perished, Israel was soundly beaten and forced to retreat beyond the Jordan, and the Philistines gained complete control of the area as far east as (and including) Beth Shan, would be a mocking insult or an expression of bitter irony, neither sentiment being

---

[17] There are exceptions to this rule (cf. GKC § 127 *f;* Gordon in *JNES* VIII [1949] 112), but the present example cannot be construed as such.

[18] H. P. Smith, *op. cit.,* pp. 260–61; S. R. Driver, *Notes on the Hebrew Text and the Topography of the Books of Samuel* (2d ed.; Oxford, 1913) pp. 234 f.

[19] Cf., *inter alia,* Isa. 16:12; BDB, p. 119 *a* (3); *Lexicon in Veteris Testamenti libros* (ed. Ludwig Koehler [Leiden, 1953]) p. 132.

consonant with the tenor of the poem. Nevertheless, with respect to the phrase
על במותיך חלל and the following איך נפלו גבורים everything points to the
soundness of the received text; the two lines are repeated farther along in the
poem (verse 25) in accordance with tradition in reverse sequence, and both the
Septuagint[20] and Targum Jonathan render the Massoretic text literally with
the same terms in each place. Either the verse became corrupt, then, before its
translation into these other languages or our understanding of the text is at
fault. The repetition of the phrases argues forcibly for the integrity of the
text, and I am therefore inclined to believe that what misunderstandings exist
have arisen from a failure to discern a nuance in the language employed.

Proceeding from the known to the less well known, we may begin with the
phrase "how the heroes have fallen!" This line, expressing the poet's shock
and profound grief at the loss of Israel's military might and, more particularly,
of Saul and Jonathan, is the refrain of this lament, for it is repeated twice again
tellingly. Both the Greek and Aramaic versions bear witness to the same text
and to the same understanding of it in each of the three occurrences.[21] Moreover, such phrasing of the dirge's refrain appears to have been traditional if
we may judge from similar constructions in analogous contexts, for example
in Jer. 9:18:

כי קול נהי נשמע מציון

א י ך   שדדנו בשנו מאד

For a sound of wailing is heard from Zion:
How we are ruined, greatly ashamed!

We find it used by Ezekiel in his lamentation over Tyre, Ezek. 26:17:

א י ך   אבדת

How thou hast perished . . .!

and in the opening dirge of the Book of Lamentations:

א י כ ה   ישבה בדד

How she doth sit solitary . . .!

Of so much then we may be certain: the text of the refrain and its meaning.

The immediately preceding prepositional phrase על במותיך חלל, however
innocent of difficulties it may on the surface appear, cannot with unequivocal
justification be rendered "on thy high places is slain" because, as we have indicated above, Gilboa, the scene of the heroes' deaths, was neither "high places"
nor Israel's.

---

[20] Except for the Lagardiana recension.

[21] Septuagint: πῶς ἔπεσαν δυνατοί; Targum Jonathan: ·איכדין אתקטלו גבריא

Of late, however, under the stimulus of Ugaritic studies, it has been recognized that the term במת in biblical Hebrew occasionally bears the meaning "back," as in Isa. 14:14:[22]

אעלה על במתי עב

I will go up on the *backs* of the cloud(s),

in which it agrees with its cognates in Ugaritic and Akkadian.[23] Through a semantic development which can be paralleled almost precisely in biblical Hebrew במת, "back," came to denote "body" and, more specifically, "dead body," "corpse."[24] This meaning has been advanced for במת in Deut. 33:29 (see references in n. 25):

ואתה על במותימו תדרך

And thou, upon their *bodies* shalt thou tread.

In addition, a phrase strikingly similar to that under discussion has appeared in the Qumran "Scroll of the War of the Sons of Light against the Sons of Darkness," col. xii 10. There, the phrase with which it is in parallel, a quotation of Gen. 49:8, establishes this proposed meaning beyond any doubt:

תן ידכה בעורף אויביכה
ורגלכה על במותי חלל

Set thy hand on the neck of thine enemies,
And thy foot on the bodies of slain.

Clearly, it will be seen, על במותי חלל contains no reference to "high places," and clearly too the passage in David's lament, in the light of the Qumran text, must be similarly understood.[25]

---

[22] Cf. Albright, *CBQ* VII 31; M. H. Pope, *EL in the Ugaritic Texts* (*VT* "Supplement" II [Leiden, 1955]) p. 102. Cf. further Job 9:8.

[23] Gordon, *UM*, § 20:332; W. von Soden, *Akkadisches Handwörterbuch* (Wiesbaden, 1959——) p. 101 *b*. For the etymology of ʙᴍᴛ, see Albright in *Volume du Congrès, Strasbourg, 1956* (*VT* "Supplement" IV [Leiden, 1957]) pp. 242 ff., particularly pp. 255–57, and B. Landsberger in *JNES* VIII (1949) 276 f., n. 91.

[24] Cf. גו , גוה = "back" and גויה = "body," "corpse."

[25] The first editor of the Qumran "War Scroll," the late Professor E. L. Sukenik, drew attention to the similarity in an apparent recognition of the relatedness of the expressions (*Megilloth Genuzoth* II [Jerusalem, 1950] 51, n.). Yigael (Sukenik) Yadin later presented a full and excellent commentary on the text. In the Hebrew edition of this work (*The Scroll of the War of the Sons of Light against the Sons of Darkness* [Jerusalem, 1955] p. 331) he too called for a comparison of the two passages; but in the English edition (London, 1962) he seems to have altered his opinion (p. 317), for he writes of the phrase in II Sam. 1:19 that it "occurs . . . in quite a different sense." Unfortunately, he has not elaborated upon this view. Nor do the remarks of Yalon in *Sinai* XXVI (5710) 285(!), to which Yadin refers, clarify the position.

Yet two problems stand menacingly in the way of so facile an interpretation. One—to which we shall return when the remainder of the second verse has been discussed—is that when this phrase is repeated in verse 25, it is immediately preceded by the personal name "Jonathan" and is syntactically united with it. The second problem is that, while in the Qumran "War Scroll" the terms במותי חלל form an uncluttered construct chain, "bodies of slain," in the dirge they are separated by the pronominal element -kā suffixed to the first of them: במותי-ך. It is here, I believe, that insensitivity to a nicety of biblical Hebrew style has effectively blocked correct interpretation of the passage. For, while the general rule is that words in construct relationship form a single complex idea, one which cannot tolerate separation of the component elements (a noun in construct and its following genitive) by intervening words or morphemes, exceptions to the rule are legion and have long been noted.[26] The intervening elements are of various kinds: the definite article,[27] case endings,[28] prepositions,[29] copulative *wāw*,[30] enclitic *mem*,[31] and, most significant in the present context, pronominal suffixes.[32] Because of the importance of this last category for the interpretation here advanced we adduce a few examples

Ps. 71:7 (1st person sing.):

ואתה מחסי עז

And thou art my refuge of strength;

[26] See GKC, §§ 127 *f*, 128, and 130; E. König, *Zeitschrift der Deutschen morgenländischen Gesellschaft* LIII (1899) 521–24; P. Joüon, *Grammaire de l'Hébreu biblique* (2e éd.; Rome, 1947) p. 386, n. 2; C. H. Gordon, *JNES* VIII (1949) 113 f., *UM*, § 8:13, *Orientalia* XXII (1953) 230, *RA* L (1956) 128, n. 2; M. M. Bravmann, *JAOS* LXXXI (1961) 386–94.

[27] GKC, § 127, and elsewhere.

[28] GKC, § 90, particularly *k–o*.

[29] GKC, § 130 *a*.   [30] GKC, § 130 *b*.

[31] On this widely discussed phenomenon in Ugaritic and in biblical Hebrew see (in addition to the remarks of Gordon cited in n. 26 above) Ginsberg in *Journal of the Royal Asiatic Society*, 1935, p. 47, *JBL* LXII (1943) 115 and LXIX (1950) 54; Albright, *JBL* LXIII (1944) 215, n. 45, and 219, n. 83, *CBQ* VII (1945) 23 f.; J. H. Patton, *Canaanite Parallels in the Book of Psalms* (Baltimore, 1944) pp. 12 f.; T. H. Gaster, *Jewish Quarterly Review* XXXVII (1946) 65, n. 32, and 58, n. 9; M. Dahood, *Biblica* XXXIII (1952) 194; J. Reider, *JJS* III (1952) 78 f. and *Hebrew Union College Annual* XXIV (1952/53) 97; A. Jirku, *Biblica* XXXIV (1953) 78–80; N. Sarna, *JJS* VI (1955) 108–10; H. D. Hummel, *JBL* LXXVI (1957) 85 ff.

[32] GKC, § 128 *d*. The phenomenon may be noted at Mari as well. Cf. *ARM* I 59:7–8: GEMÉ-*sú I-túr-ás-du-ú*! (*amassu Itūr-asdu*), "the maid-servant of PN" (lit.: "his maid-servant of PN"). For the corrected reading of this personal name see *ARM* II 240 and *ARM* XV 150. For analysis of it as in the genitive case cf. *a-na Ḫa-aq-ba-ḫa-am-mu* (*ARM* II 39:80), *aš-šum Za-ak-ku-ú* (*ARM* II 63:30), *it-ti I-zi-[n]a-bu-ú* (*ARM* II 128:11), etc. For another explanation of the indeclinability of certain personal names see André Finet, *L'Accadien des lettres de Mari* (Bruxelles, 1956) p. 82, § 33 *b*.

Ezek. 16:27 (2d fem. sing.):

מדרכך זמה

From thy path of lewdness;

Ezek. 18:7 (3d masc. sing.):

חבלתו חוב

His pledge of debt;

Prov. 14:13 (3d fem. sing.):

ואחריתה שמחה

And its end of joy (=and joy's end).

In the light of these instances of the construction and of the fact of the construct relationship of במותי חלל in the "War Scroll," במותיך חלל must be recognized as such another example of a construct chain separated by a pronominal suffix. Since the rendering of במותי חלל as "bodies of slain" cannot be doubted, that of במותיך חלל must be "thy bodies of slain" (="thy slain bodies") or something very similar.

Turning now to the remaining and most difficult phrase of this verse, הצבי ישראל, we see that what is required is a verb in the imperative mood,[33] a direction to do something "on/over thy slain bodies," which "something" is probably (though not necessarily) the enunciation of the refrain: "How the heroes have fallen!" Both Septuagint's στήλωσον and Targum Jonathan's אתעתדתון point directly and unequivocally to a text which read not הַצְּבִי, "the gazelle," but הַצֵּב(וֹ), "erect," or "raise up," and this, in all probability, is what we must read. If the term "Israel" in its present position is original and the subject of the verb, then we must assume that the object, the word designating what was to be "raised," has dropped completely from the text. But it may perhaps be ventured that "Israel" hides some term for "wail," "lament," "dirge," or the like, possibly אבל or אליה.[34]

Understood in this manner the second verse of the lament would read:

הצב(ו) 'אליה / אבל' על במותיך חלל
איך נפלו גבורים

Raise up a dirge over thy bodies of slain:
How the heroes have fallen!

[33] Note the prohibitives in the following verse: אל תגידו, "do not tell," and אל תבשרו, "do not proclaim!"

[34] For this use of the verb NṢB cf. Ps. 119:89. One is furthermore tempted to emend ישראל to read שיר אל(יה), "song of lament." However, it must be noted that the noun אליה, known in post-biblical Hebrew, is unknown in biblical Hebrew (though a verbal form

When the phrase על במותיך חלל is repeated in verse 25, we find it preceded by what appears quite evidently to be the personal name Jonathan; but,
again, what is required is a verb in the imperative mood plus an object of that
verb which would constitute what is to be done "on/over thy bodies of slain."
The name Jonathan in its present position, it would therefore appear, represents a corruption of these required elements. The first part of the name, יהו,
we would guess to be a simple scribal error for יהי, the jussive, "let there be!"
And as for the remainder, נתן, Ginsberg in his commentary on the Ugaritic
text *Keret*,[35] pointed out that a term *ntn* twice substitutes for *bky*, "weeping,"
and must therefore bear the same or a similar meaning, whatever its etymology
may prove to be.[36] We would therefore suggest that, however rare, the term
ntn was alive in both Ugaritic and biblical Hebrew, that it bore the meaning
"mourning (cry)" or the like, and that in verse 25 of our text יהונתן may
originally have read יהי נתן, "let it be a mourning (cry)."

III

Following his call to lament, the poet, as though he could himself enforce
it, utters a prohibition forbidding proclamation of the news of Israel's defeat
in the Philistine cities:

אל תגידו בגת

אל תבשרו בחוצת אשקלון

Do not tell (of it) in Gath,
Do not proclaim (it as good tidings) in the streets of Ashkelon!

Of the elements here set in parallel the verbs may be singled out as being of
particular interest, for David makes similar use of them in II Sam. 4:10:

כי ה-מ ג י ד לי לאמר הנה מת שאול

והוא היה כ-מ ב ש ר בעיניו ....

When *he who told* me saying, "Behold, Saul is dead"—
And he was as a *proclaimer* (of good tidings) in his eyes. . . .

---

occurs in Joel 1:8), and while שרים and שרות, "singers," may perform laments (cf. II Chron.
35:25), the noun שיר, "song," in biblical Hebrew regularly signifies a song of joy rather than
of sorrow.

[35] *The Legend of King Keret*, p. 44.

[36] It may, perhaps, be suggested that such etymology is to be sought along with that of the
biblical Hebrew verb תנה. The *piʿēl* infinitive of this verb appears in Judg. 11:40, where it
is rendered in the Septuagint θρηνεῖν and in Targum Jonathan לאלאה, i.e., "to mourn."
Note that, as in the Ugaritic passage referred to immediately above, so in the biblical passage, there is an interchange with the verb בכה (Judg. 11:37 ff.).

They are associated again in II Kings 7:9 and Isa. 41:26–27, while the difference in meaning between these verbs is subtly but brilliantly exploited in II Sam. 18:19 ff.

Of the remaining terms only the names of the cities Gath and Ashkelon are clearly in parallel. Nevertheless, one senses a curious imbalance in the lines; for, while it is not uncommon in Hebrew poetry to have more terms in one line than in its parallel, it is most unusual in such strictly synonymous parallelism for the second of the two cola to contain a significant element without a correspondent term in the first. Despite the evidence of Mic. 1:10,[37] therefore, there is lacking in the first colon a word for which חוצת serves as a parallel in the second. Seeking an appropriate term with which to balance the lines, we find that the regular, we may say fixed, correspondent of חוצות, "streets," in biblical poetry is רחבות, "plazas." The pair occurs nine times,[38]

for example in Jer. 9:20*b:*

$$\text{להכרית עולל מ-חוץ}$$
$$\text{בחורים מ-רחבות}$$

To cut off children from the *street*(s),
Young men from the *plazas,*

Nah. 2:5*a:*

$$\text{ב-חוצות יתהוללו הרכב}$$
$$\text{ישתקשקון ב-רחבות}$$

In the *streets* the chariots rumble madly,
They scramble about in the *plazas,*

Prov. 1:20:

$$\text{חכמות ב-חוצ(ת) רנה}$$
$$\text{ב-רחבות תתן קולה}$$

Wisdom crieth out in the *streets,*[39]
In the *plazas* giveth forth her voice.

It is therefore likely that our text read originally:

$$\text{אל תגידו ב⟨רחבות⟩ גת}$$
$$\text{אל תבשרו בחוצת אשקלון}$$

Do not tell (of it) in ⸢the plazas⸣ of Gath,
Do not proclaim (it as good tidings) in the streets of Ashkelon!

[37] ‏בגת אל תגידו‎.

[38] Isa. 15:3; Jer. 5:1, 9:20; Amos 5:16; Nah. 2:5; Prov. 1:20, 5:16, 7:12, 22:13. Cf. also Ps. 144:13–14.

[39] On this reading cf., *inter alia, BH, ad loc.* n.

If so, the poet, for reasons unknown, reversed the traditional order of terms. This particular sequence, however, is supported by another occurrence, Amos 5:16aβ:

בכל רחבות מספד

ובכל חוצות יאמרו הו הו

In all *plazas* (there shall be) mourning,
And in all *streets* they shall say, "Woe! Woe!"

IV

As his reason for the prohibition the poet gives that the Philistine women would otherwise gloat over Israel's defeat:

פן תשמחנה בנות פלשתים

פן תעלזנה בנות הערלים

Lest the daughters of the Philistines be glad,
Lest the daughters of the uncircumcised rejoice.

In constructing this line he has again made use of a fixed parallel pair, "be glad" // "rejoice." It is found again in

Prov. 23:15–16:

בני אם חכם לבך ישמח לבי גם אני

ו-תעלזנה כליותי בדבר שפתיך מישרים

My son, if thy heart be wise, my heart shall be *glad*, even I,
And my inwards shall *rejoice* when thy lips speak proprieties;

Jer. 50:11:

כי תשמחי

כי תעלזי

Though you be *glad*,
Though you *rejoice;*

Zeph. 3:14*a:*

שמחי ו-עלזי בכל לב

Be *glad* and *rejoice* with all (thy) heart.

For the parallelism "Philistines" // "uncircumcised" note the interchange of these terms in the statements of Jonathan in I Sam. 14:1 and 6.

V

Still in a negative frame of mind the poet turns to the scene of the Israelite heroes' fall and, addressing the mountains of Gilboa, with vituperation damns them to infertility:

הרי בגלבע⁴⁰

אל טל

ואל מטר עליכם

ושדי תרומת

Mountains of Gilboa:⁴⁰
No dew
And no rain be upon you,
. . . .

The major textual problem in this verse is the final line, here left untranslated. Rendered literally it reads:

And fields of offerings.

This line has long been recognized as a *crux interpretum*, the phrase as strange, and the literal translation of it as quite without meaning in the context.

The verse in its entirety, it would nevertheless seem, is based firmly on tradition. We may note first that the parallelism of the terms טל // מטר, "dew" // "rain," is found twice again in Old Testament poetry, though in reverse sequence, Deut. 32:2*a:*

יערף כ-מ ט ר לקחי

תזל כ-ט ל אמרתי

May my teaching drop as the *rain,*
May my speech distil as the *dew,*

and Job 38:28:

היש ל-מ ט ר אב

או מי הוליד אגלי ט ל

Hath the *rain* a father?
Or, who hath begotten the drops(?) of *dew?*

Since the poet is here concerned to prevent, by means of his imprecation, the fructifying waters from reaching the scene of the slaughter, it is reasonable to suppose that the final line also contains reference to a source of water and that the association of all three terms is a further aspect of his poetic tradition. Now of all the attempts at elucidating the last colon the most attractive is that of Ginsberg,⁴¹ who drew attention to the closely parallel Ugaritic text

⁴⁰ This is an example of a preposition intervening between a noun in the construct state and its following genitive. This syntactical phenomenon is too well attested in biblical Hebrew to warrant emending the present text. Cf. p. 80 above and GKC, § 130 *a.* To the examples there cited may perhaps be added II Sam. 10:9 (Kethib).

⁴¹ *JBL* LVII (1938) 213.

UM 1 Aqht 44–45:

בל טל

בל רבב!

בל שרע תהמתמ

No dew,
No rain,
No upsurging[42] of the deep(s),

and very plausibly suggested seeing in ושדי תרומת a corruption of שרע
תהומ(ו)ת.[43] The "deeps" are the underground waters and are precisely what the
imprecation requires. Reconstructing the third colon in this manner, we find
that the major difference between the Ugaritic and Hebrew texts lies in their
respective words for "rain." But just as טל // מטר is found elsewhere in
biblical poetry, so too may we note the parallelism טל // רבב in Mic. 5:6αβ:

כ-ט ל מאת יהוה

כ-ר ב י ב י ם עלי עשב

Like *dew* from YHWH,
Like *showers* upon grass(?).[44]

[42] For *šrˁ*, "upsurge," Ginsberg has compared Arabic *šrˁ*, "to hasten." (May Syriac *šrˁ*,
"to slip," "to slide," be enlisted?) For Ugaritic *šrˁ* = Akkadian *šurrû*, "to reach the water
crest," see E. A. Speiser, *JBL* LXIX (1950) 378.

[43] *JBL* LVII 213; *ANET*, p. 153, n. 34.

[44] Cf. Cassuto, *The Goddess Anath*, p. 79, but read instead:

כטל מאת יהוה

כרביב(ים?) מעלי

Like dew from YHWH,
Like shower(s) from ˁLY,

with which compare *UM* 126 III 5–8:

לאַרץ מטר בעל

ולשד מטר עלי

נעמ לאַרץ מטר בעל

ולשד מטר עלי

Unto the earth raineth Baal,
And unto the field raineth ˁLY;
Pleasant to the earth is the rain of Baal,
And to the field the rain of ˁLY.

On ˁLY as a divine name or epithet in Ugaritic and in biblical Hebrew, see particularly M.
Dahood in *Theological Studies* XIV (1953) 452–57. To the earlier studies cited there add

And for טל // תהומות, compare Prov. 3:20:

בדעתו תהומות נבקעו
ושחקים ירעפו ט ל

By his knowledge the *deeps* break out,
And the clouds drop *dew*.

Of importance also, as Ginsberg has indicated, is the fact that the two texts are furthermore alike in that the wish in each case has been prompted by the news of the (violent) death of the heroes.[45] This tradition, moreover, of condemning the scene of slaughter with lack of fertilizing waters appears to have lived on, if we may judge from a similar response found in a pre-Islamic poem. The text relates of a sole survivor of a battle who curses the place where his comrades fell. It was published by Julius Wellhausen,[46] who, conscious of its relation to the biblical passage, rendered the imprecation *lā suqiyat ʾAmūlu* somewhat freely as ". . . möge weder Tau noch Regen auf Umul fallen"; but it should be rendered more exactly ". . . may Amulu not be watered" or ". . . may Amulu not be rained upon!" Nevertheless, the relationship between these is clear, and the poetic tradition from which they stem evidently similar. In view of the central role played by tradition in the construction of early Hebrew verse, what differences exist between the Ugaritic and biblical passages are certainly minor, and we may unhesitatingly adopt Ginsberg's reading, rendering the verse:

No dew
And no rain be upon you,
(No) upsurging of the deeps!

VII

Having thus vented his feelings of guilt with an angry curse upon the scene of Saul's and Jonathan's demise, David can more easily express his feelings of loss.[47] This he does with a compassion born of a world view shared with those he laments: the manly, heroic world of war and physical prowess. For him

---

those of Paul Ruben, "Strophic Forms in the Bible," *Jewish Quarterly Review* XI (1898–99) 446, and G. R. Driver, "Hebrew ʿal ('high one') as a Divine Title," *The Expository Times* L (1938) 92 f.

[45] *JBL* LVII 213.

[46] *Skizzen und Vorarbeiten* I (Berlin, 1844) p. 139, No. 189.

[47] This would appear, in general, to be the effect also of II Sam. 1:21*b*, our division VI, but the text is obscure at several points of detail. For the lexical difficulties see the commentaries. Note, in addition, the apparently rambling and quite uncertain structure of the parallelism. I am unable at present either to accept any of the solutions proposed or to offer any satisfactory alternative.

Saul and Jonathan embodied these virtues, and his praise is unrestrained:

מדם חללים(?)

מחלב גבורים

קשת יהונתן לא נשוג אחור

וחרב שאול לא תשוב ריקם

From the blood of the slain(?)
From the fat of the heroes,
The bow of Jonathan turned not back,
The sword of Saul returned not empty.

Employing the fixed parallel pair דם // חלב, "blood" // "fat," David has here created a powerful image, for the association of these terms in biblical Hebrew regularly connotes sacrifice,

Isa. 34:6:

חרב ליהוה מלאה ד ם

הדשנה מ- ח ל ב

מ- ד ם כרים ועתודים

מ- ח ל ב כליות אילים

Yhwh's sword is glutted with *blood*,
Greased with *fat*—
With the *blood* of lambs and goats,
With the *fat* of the kidneys of rams,

Lev. 7:33:

המקריב את ד ם השלמים

ואת ה- ח ל ב מבני אהרן

And the one from among the sons of Aaron who offereth the *blood* of the peace-offerings and the *fat* (shall have the right thigh for a portion),

Isa. 1:11:

שבעתי עלות אילים ו- ח ל ב מריאים

ו- ד ם פרים וכבשים ועתודים לא חפצתי

I am sated with holocausts of rams and the *fat* of fed cattle,
And the *blood* of bulls and lambs and goats I desire not.

David has here, then, made of the military accomplishments of Saul and Jonathan something other even than soldierly skills and courage worthy of the highest praise; he has likened their deeds to the performance of a sacrifice and thereby has transformed them into an act of worship.

Although the phrase "blood of the slain" is known elsewhere,[48] in its present

[48] Num. 23:24, Deut. 32:42, and cf. Job 39:30.

context it is inappropriate and quite evidently inconsistent with the praise intended. Furthermore, it cannot be said of the parallelism "slain" // "heroes," occurring only here, as it can of "blood" // "fat," that it is particularly apt or poetically synonymous. However, a not infrequent pair in biblical Hebrew poetry, graphically close to the present text, appears to have been חיל // גבורים. To the former element, חיל, "strength," "valor," consistently found as the second of the pair, there is regularly appended a noun in the construct state, either "men (of valor)" or "son(s) of valor),"[49] for example

Isa. 5:22:

הוי גבורים לשתות יין
ו-אנשי חיל למסך שכר

Woe to the *heroes* at drinking wine,
And (to) the *men of valor* at mixing beer,

Jer. 48:14:

איך תאמרו גבורים אנחנו
ו-אנשי חיל למלחמה

How can you say, "We are *heroes*,"
"And *men of valor* with respect to battle"?

Nah. 2:4*aa*:

מגן גבריהו מאדם
אנשי חיל מתלעים

The shield of his *heroes* is reddened,
The *men of valor* are scarleted,

II Sam. 17:10*b*:

כי גבור אביך
ו-בני חיל אשר אתו

For a *hero* is thy father,
And *sons of valor* are those with him.

We noted above (pp. 36–38) that, when a traditional sequence of a fixed pair of parallel terms is inverted in biblical poetry, to that term regularly found as the first of the pair, now set as the second, another element frequently is added. This suggests the possibility that the traditional pair may have been חַיִל* // גבור, "valiant (one)" // "hero," and that in David's poem this pair is to be reconstructed. That is to say, instead of the received text's:

> From the blood of the slain (חללים)
> From the fat of the heroes (גבורים),

---

[49] Cf. further the Qumran "War Scroll," cols. xii 9–10 and xix 2–3.

we should probably read:

From the blood of the valiant (חֲיָלִים)[50]

From the fat of the heroes (גבורים).

The emendation is slight, the tradition would be sound, the parallelism appropriate, and the praise more worthy and consistent.

The second couplet is composed of three sets of parallelisms: "bow" // "sword," the names "Jonathan" // "Saul," and the phrases "turned not back" // "returned not empty." The first of these is a fixed pair in biblical poetry, occurring seven more times,[51] for example

Ps. 44:7:

כי לא ב-קשתי אבטח

ו-חרבי לא תושיעני

For not in my *bow* do I trust,
Nor shall my *sword* save me,

Isa. 41:2bβ:

יתן כעפר חרבו

כקש נדף קשתו

He maketh them like dust with his *sword*,
Like driven chaff with his *bow*.

Although the parallelism of the personal names "Jonathan" // "Saul" cannot be said to constitute a fixed pair, nevertheless the poet manipulates them as though they did; in the following verse, forming of them a compound subject, he reverses their sequence.

The two phrases comprising the last of this couplet's pairs do not recur in parallel. Each of them separately, however, may be regarded as a "formulaic phrase" (see pp. 11 f.), since the first, "turned (not) back," occurs eleven more times,[52] for example

Isa. 50:5:

My lord Yнwн opened my ear
And I, I did not rebel,
I turned not back (אחור לא נסוגתי),

---

[50] Cf. Akkadian (Neo-Babylonian) ʟúḫa-a-a-laᴍᴇš etc. (For reference see W. von Soden, *Akkadisches Handwörterbuch*, p. 342).

[51] In the sequence found in David's lament: Ps. 44:7 and 76:4. In reverse sequence: Isa. 21:15, 41:2; Ps. 7:13, 37:14 and 15. In prose, cf. Gen. 48:22, Josh. 24:12, I Sam. 18:4, II Kings 6:22. And note also Hos. 1:7 and 2:20.

[52] Isa. 42:17, 50:5, 59:13–14; Jer. 38:22, 46:5; Zeph. 1:6; Ps. 35:4, 40:15 (=70:3), 44:19, 129:5.

Ps. 44:19:

Our heart hath not turned back (לא נסוג אחור),
(Nor) our steps departed from thy way,

and the second, "returned not empty," twice again,

Isa. 55:11:

So shall be my word which hath gone forth from my mouth, it shall not return unto me empty (לא ישוב אלי ריקם);

Jer. 50:9*b*:

His arrows are like an able hero who returneth not empty (לא ישוב ריקם).

VIII

Still within the framework of his literary tradition, the poet, in verse 23, continues his praise:

שאול ויהונתן

הנאהבים והנעימם

Saul and Jonathan—
The beloved and the pleasant!

For just as the sequence of the names Saul and Jonathan here reverses that of the same names in the immediately preceding verse, so too the present sequence of "(be)love(d)" and "pleasant" is farther on (verse 26) reversed.

The traditional pointing of the following colon has long been questioned. The Massoretic text reads:

הנאהבים והנעימם בחייהם

ובמותם לא נפרדו

The beloved and the pleasant in their lives,
And in their death they were not divided,

with a *zāqēf qāṭōn* over the word for "their lives," while most modern scholars would read:

In their lives and in their death they were not divided.

That a difficulty exists is apparent. The difficulty would seem to lie in the absence of a verb, an appropriate correspondent of "were not divided," suggested both by the regularity of the use of poetic parallelism in early Hebrew verse and by the appearance in the Septuagint of both οὐ διακεχωρισμένοι and οὐ διακεχωρίσθησαν. No fixed parallel of פרד, "to divide," is evident, and no certain reconstruction therefore can as yet be advanced with confidence; but the negatived verb occurs in parallel with דבק (or, less likely, לכד), "to cling," "to join," in Job 41:9 (Eng. 41:17):

אִישׁ בְּאָחִיהוּ יְדֻבָּקוּ

יִתְלַכְּדוּ וְ־לֹא יִתְפָּרָדוּ

They are *joined* one with another (lit.: his brother)
They clasp and are *not divided*,

and we may perhaps suggest a similar parallelism in our passage, so that it
would read:

שָׁאוּל וִיהוֹנָתָן

הַנֶּאֱהָבִים וְהַנְּעִימִם

בְּחַיֵּיהֶם ⟨דְּבֵקוּ/הִתְלַכְּדוּ⟩

וּבְמוֹתָם לֹא נִפְרָדוּ

Saul and Jonathan—
The beloved and the pleasant!
In their lives ⟨they were joined⟩
And in their death they were not divided.

IX

In the final couplet of verse 23 the poet exalts the physical prowess of the
two whose death he laments:

מִנְּשָׁרִים קַלּוּ

מֵאֲרָיוֹת גָּבֵרוּ

They were swifter than eagles,
They were stronger than lions.

The analogy "swifter than eagles" recurs in Jer. 4:13 and in Lam. 4:19. Of
considerably more interest is the parallelism גבר // קלל, "swift" // "strong,"
that may be noted again in Jer. 46:6*a:*

אַל יָנוּס הַ־קַּל

וְאַל יִמָּלֵט הַ־גִּבּוֹר

The *swift* shall not flee away,
Nor shall the *strong* escape,

and in Eccl. 9:11:

כִּי לֹא לַ־קַּלִּים הַמֵּרוֹץ

וְלֹא לַ־גִּבּוֹרִים הַמִּלְחָמָה

For the race is not to the *swift*,
Nor the battle to the *strong*.

Most striking of all, perhaps, is the use of the terms of this parallelism indi-
vidually at the two ends of the biblical "Flood Story." In Gen. 7:18 (cf. also

verses 19, 20, and 24) the verb used to designate the increase of the waters is
גבר. We read:

ו - י ג ב ר ו   ה מ י ם

And the waters became mighty. . . .

And in Gen. 8:11 (cf. also verse 8) the verb used to designate the recession of
the waters is קלל. We read:

וידע נח כי ק ל ו   ה מ י ם

And Noah knew that the waters had receded. . . .

We called attention above (pp. 62 f.) to the same phenomenon—the use of
each of the terms of a traditionally parallel pair at each of the two extremes of
a prose account—and argued, as we would now reiterate, that such use can
be not the result of accident but only of deliberate artistry.[53]

X

David then turns to the women of Israel, recipients of Saul's bounty, ex-
horting them to bewail the war chief who decked them so magnanimously
with finery from his battle-won spoils:

בנות ישראל אל שאול בכינה

המלבשכם שני עם עדנים(?)

המעלה עדי זהב על לבושכן

Daughters of Israel, weep over[54] Saul!
Who clothed you in scarlet (raiment) with dainties(?),
Who put adornments of gold upon your apparel.

That the parallelism "scarlet (raiment)" // "adornments of gold" was traditional in Hebrew verse is indicated by Jeremiah's similar employment of it,
Jer. 4:30*aa*:

ואתי שדוד מה תעשי

כי תלבשי ש נ י

כי תעדי ע ד י   ז ה ב

And thou, desolate one, what dost thou,
That thou clothest thyself in *scarlet* (raiment),
That thou adornest thyself with *adornments of gold?*

Scholars have long remarked the unsuitability of the term עדנים, "dainties," in a context which requires rather an article of dress. This long-standing

[53] The theory of a poetic substratum underlying the narratives of Genesis, advocated by
Cassuto (*From Adam to Noah* [trans. by I. Abrahams; Jerusalem, 1961] *passim*), is thus given
some additional support.
[54] Cf. II Sam. 3:33.

objection to the received text finds oblique support in the observation that the parallelism "dainties" // "apparel," in addition to being awkward, is otherwise unknown. Some would emend the term in question to סדינים, "(fine) linen,"[55] while others,[56] in accordance with the rendering in the Septuagint, μετὰ κοσμου ὑμῶν, would emend it to עדיכן or to עדיים. The latter is doubtless the original reading; for, in addition to the evidence of the Greek translation, we may note the recurrence of the parallelism עדה // לבש, "to clothe" // "to adorn," found for example in the text quoted above (Jer. 4:30):

כי תלבשי שני

כי תעדי עדי זהב

That thou *clothest* thyself in scarlet (raiment),
That thou *adornest* thyself with adornments of gold,

and Job 40:10:[57]

עדה נא גאון וגבה

והוד והדר תלבש

Adorn thyself, pray, with majesty and dignity,
And with glory and splendor *clothe* thyself.

Thus supported by the evidence both of the Septuagint and of the tradition of poetic parallelism, we may with confidence read:

המלבשכם שני עם עדיים

המעלה עדי זהב על לבושכן

Who clothed you in scarlet (raiment) with (your?) adornments,
Who put adornments of gold upon your apparel,

noting, furthermore, that the sequence of terms in the first colon is clothing with adornments, and in the second, adornments upon clothing.

XI

Having admonished the women of Israel to mourn for Saul and having, thereby, praised him for his generosity, David repeats the refrain of his lament (see p. 82 on reading of final line):

איך נפלו גברים

בתוך המלחמה

יהי נתן על במותיך חלל

How the heroes have fallen!
In the midst of the battle—
Let it be a mourning (cry) over thy bodies of slain!

---

[55] E.g., H. P. Smith, *A Critical and Exegetical Commentary on the Books of Samuel*, p. 263.
[56] E.g., G. A. Smith, *The Historical Geography of the Holy Land* (26th ed.; London, 1935) p. 404.
[57] Cf. also Ezek. 16:13.

XII

Just as the Israelite women who had benefited from Saul's munificence were called upon to weep, so David mourns, confessing the gift of Jonathan's friendship:

צר לי עליך אחי יהונתן

נעמת לי מאד

נפלאתה אהבתך לי מאהבת נשים

I am distressed over thee, my brother, Jonathan—
Exceedingly pleasant wast thou to me;
More wonderful was thy love to me than the love of women.

XIII

And just as following his praise of Saul the poet repeated his refrain, so after this praise of Jonathan does he intone it, summing up his feelings, his evaluation of the heroes, and his lament:

איך נפלו גבורים

ויאבדו כלי מלחמה

How the heroes have fallen!
And the instruments of war perished!

The word כלי, a general term for "finished article," is used to signify such diverse items as censers, utensils, and the like and bears the meaning "weapon(s)" when, as here, it stands in construct relation with "battle," that is to say, "instruments of battle" = "weapons." Here, of course, the poet has proceeded one step further in his analogy, for Saul and Jonathan are themselves the perished instruments of war.

TRANSLATION OF THE RECONSTRUCTED TEXT

   I. (With) a bitter wailing, weep O Judah!
      (With) a grievous lament, mourn O Israel!
  II. Raise up a dirge over thy bodies of slain:
      How the heroes have fallen!
 III. Do not tell (of it) in the plazas of Gath,
      Do not proclaim (it as good tidings) in the streets of Ashkelon!
 IV. Lest the daughters of the Philistines be glad,
      Lest the daughters of the uncircumcised rejoice.
  V. Mountains of Gilboa:
      No dew
      And no rain be upon you,
      (No) upsurging of the deeps!
 VI. . . . .
      . . . .

VII. From the blood of the valiant,
From the fat of the heroes,
The bow of Jonathan turned not back,
And the sword of Saul returned not empty.

VIII. Saul and Jonathan—
The beloved and the pleasant!
In their lives they were joined
And in their death they were not divided.

IX. They were swifter than eagles,
They were stronger than lions.

X. Daughters of Israel, weep over Saul!
Who clothed you in scarlet (raiment) with adornments,
Who put adornments of gold upon your apparel.

XI. How the heroes have fallen!
In the midst of the battle—
Let it be a mourning (cry) over thy bodies of slain!

XII. I am distressed over thee, my brother, Jonathan—
Exceedingly pleasant wast thou to me,
More wonderful was thy love to me than the love of women.

XIII. How the heroes have fallen!
And the instruments of war perished!

EPILOGUE

IN THE preceding pages we have endeavored to demonstrate the early Hebrew poets' dependence upon, and artful employment of, a traditional literary diction. In laying bare some of these basic elements of their craft, our avowed intent throughout has been to bring into sharper focus some of the less obvious meanings attendant upon their literary constructions and thereby to excite a greater appreciation for their poetic compositions qua poems.

We began these studies with what appeared to us to be a verifiable and self-evident truth: the pervasiveness of a tradition in the fashioning of early Hebrew poetry. This Syro-Palestinian tradition to which the biblical poets were heir, which seems to have had its origins in remote antiquity and which may have been motivated, we suggested, by the requirements of oral verse formation, consisted for the most part in the employment of fixed pairs of words set in parallel structure. Through a close investigation of five poems we set out to examine the use made of this tradition by the early Hebrew poets and the applicability of the resultant patterns as a literary-critical tool for the elucidation of the meaning of these several texts.

Hopefully, we may have met with some success; hopefully, too, other and more significant patterns may yet be discovered, other and more significant techniques for their examination be more clearly delineated to the end that a fuller understanding of the biblical text may be ours. Whether these initial and necessarily tentative analyses, reconstructions, and interpretations may ever gain scholarly assent, that is to say, whether they may ever in all their detail stand the test of scholarly scrutiny and judgment, is now of little moment and, indeed, attenuates to insignificance before the looming centrality of our emphasis: the literary craftsmanship of the biblical poets. To be indifferent toward their art is to risk indifference for their meaning.

INDICES

I. Index of Biblical Passages Discussed

II. Index of Ugaritic Passages Discussed

III. Index of Parallel Pairs (Hebrew and Ugaritic)